C000244942

Seduction,
Surrender, and Transformation

RELATIONAL PERSPECTIVES BOOK SERIES

Volume 13

RELATIONAL PERSPECTIVES BOOK SERIES

STEPHEN A. MITCHELL AND LEWIS ARON
Series Editors

Seduction, Surrender, and Transformation

Emotional Engagement in the Analytic Process

Karen J. Maroda

THE ANALYTIC PRESS

1999   Hillsdale, NJ   London

© 1998 by The Analytic Press, Inc., Publishers

First paperback printing 2002.

All rights reserved. No part of this book may be reproduced in any form: by
photostat, microform, retrieval system, or any other means, without the prior written
permission of the publisher.

Published by The Analytic Press, Inc.
101 West Street, Hillsdale, NJ 07642
www.analyticpress.com

Typeset by in Goudy Old Style 11/13 by Qualifax, Bloomfield, NJ
Index by Leonard Rosenbaum, Washington, DC

Library of Congress Cataloguing-in-Publication Data

Maroda, Karen J.
            Seduction, surrender, and transformation : emotional engagement in the
analytic process / Karen J. Maroda
                    p. cm.
        Includes bibliographical references and index.
        ISBN 0-88163-397-6
    1. Psychotherapist and patient. 2. Psychoanalysis. I. Title.
RC480.8M37   2002
616..89'17--dc21

for Library of Congress   98-50500
                                                            CIP

Printed in the United States of America
10 9 8 7 6 5 4 3 2

Contents

To my parents, Jean and Frank Maroda

Acknowledgments

I want to thank Lew Aron for his tremendously generous support, which includes the invitation to participate in the Relational Book Series, and his careful reading and critiquing of the first draft of this manuscript. I am also thankful for his ongoing collegial encouragement and his appreciation for my ideas and ambitions. Lew Aron is that rare individual who views his colleagues not as competitors, but as collaborators in the advancement of psychoanalytic theory and practice. I also want to thank Stephen Mitchell, co-editor of this series, who has supported my work over the past few years, particularly in encouraging me to listen to my own voice, even if it strayed from the politically correct.

Practicing in Milwaukee does not provide me with many analytic colleagues and I greatly value my national support network, which includes not only Lew and Steve, but also the women of Section III, Women, Gender & Psychoanalysis, who invited me to join the board several years ago and whose members have offered their ongoing friendship, collaboration, and enthusiasm. It's nice to know that even when you have the misfortune of speaking at the same time as a star-studded panel of internationally-known analysts, there will always be some familiar faces in the audience.

I also want to thank Joe Reppen, who has probably done more to further my career than anyone else. Since inviting me to contribute to *Psychoanalytic Books* many years ago, I have done countless reviews in that journal, and have been offered opportunities to write as a result of Joe's faith in both my ideas and my ability to communicate them. He is always there for me, ready to discuss any idea or potential project, always with an openness and intellectual virtuosity that are invaluable to me.

It goes without saying that I am grateful to my patients for continuing to educate me about the therapeutic process and myself. I want particularly to thank the patients referred to in this book, especially "Susan," who gave me permission to write about them and who read and critiqued what I wrote, letting me know when I had missed the mark.

Lastly, I want to thank my partner, Nicole Horvath, for endless hours of listening to my ideas for this book and for her many creative contributions to my thinking, including the question from chapter one that she posed to me: Does psychoanalysis exist without the bad mother? She has inspired me to break out of my established ways of looking at things, constantly challenging me to see the world in new and different ways.

Introduction

The reconceptualization of the psychoanalytic situation as a two-person event has caused dramatic upheaval in the analytic world. As we struggle to understand the many nuances associated with the transition from a one-person psychology to a two-person psychology, we naturally resist change as much as we embrace it.

The refrain of "This is nothing new—psychoanalysis has always accounted ably for both the intrapsychic and the interpersonal" has become a recognizably feeble attempt to maintain the status quo. Historically, the same was said about developments in self-psychology, infant research, feminist perspectives, the frequency and impact of early trauma, and the critical importance of countertransference.

Happily, those who want to cling to the past and keep psychoanalysis the same are in the minority. The clinical experience and research evidence accumulated over the past fifty years have given birth to new theories of individual development and, as a result, a new theory of psychoanalysis. And this new understanding of the role of mutuality has breathed fresh air and excitement into an analytic discipline moving dangerously close to extinction.

The problem confronting analytic theorists and clinicians today is not *whether* to change analytic theory and practice, but *how* to change them.

1

For many years we have attempted to integrate new discoveries, particularly pertaining to countertransference and mutuality, within the existing
analytic paradigm. The goal of treatment remained similar to that expressed by Freud over seventy years ago: making the unconscious conscious, and diminishing or eliminating the transference. And the main
technical device used to achieve this goal was said to be interpretation.

As I pointed out previously (Maroda, 1991), as new discoveries were
made there were years of vain attempts to ward off any threat to the
analytic status quo. Everything began to be packaged and re-packaged as
a "form of interpretation," until we finally admitted that we could no
longer stuff the rounded repertoire of confrontation, questioning, emot-
ing, empathizing and silence into the rather squared-off realm of interpretation. To my mind, it was a great relief when people started admitting,
in print, that while the ultimate goal of analysis remained centered on
self-awareness and integration, we were not limited to interpretation as
the primary clinical tool for facilitating self-knowledge.

As the two-person psychologies take hold, with their emphasis on early
mother-child formative interactions, analysis struggles to redefine itself.
Predictably, there is much variety in thinking, even among those who
endorse the transition from viewing the analyst as an objective facilitator
of the patient's experience to viewing him as a subjective participant who,
with the patient, mutually creates the emotional reality between them.
Aron (1996) has done an admirable job of documenting the history of
the two-person perspective, beginning with Sullivan and the interpersonalists in the United States and the object-relations theorists in Britain.
He follows the course of the literature, including intersubjectivity (Stolorow and Atwood, 1992), social-constructivism (Hoffman, 1991, 1992)
and relational analysis (Mitchell, 1988), and the political climate that
allows or suppresses the development of new theoretical constructs. I
refer the reader to his scholarly review of the literature for a stimulating
historical perspective of the transition from a one-person to a two-person
approach to analysis.

As these new theories have developed over the last ten years, their
proponents have struggled both with each other and with those who
advocate the one-person perspective. Many have looked at the pluralism
of psychoanalysis and attempted to tie the seemingly divergent theories
to each other. One attempt to accomplish this goal were the "Con-

gresses," which brought analysts from all over the world to discuss not just their differences, but their commonalities. The results were reported in Wallerstein's *The Common Ground of Psychoanalysis.*

In his book Wallerstein (1992) attempts to find common ground in the many theoretical schools, noting that each contains some element of truth, some being more universal than others. Complicating the picture further, he notes that different analysts practice differently with different patients, and that an effective intervention is one that somehow speaks to the emotional experience of the patient.

What each theoretical viewpoint and personal approach to technique has in common is this: the attempt to confront defenses, reduce resistance, interpret the transference, and facilitate insight and understanding. Traditionally, making the unconscious conscious and minimizing the transference (Stone, 1961) were the goals of psychoanalysis. However, this definition no longer serves us because it remains a definition based on analysis as an intrapsychic rather than both an intrapsychic and interpersonal event. A two-person psychoanalysis requires a new definition that accounts for the transference-countertransference interplay and the roles of two active participants.

Sometimes the notion of mutuality seems to imply that both the analyst and the patient are in treatment together. This is not true, although it is unlikely that the treatment will be successful unless the analyst does change to some extent. But I will explore that point later. As analysis begins, the analyst is still in the authoritative position of doing an assessment and deciding, in a dialogue with the patient, what he or she hopes to achieve in the course of the analysis. But rather than simply noting how the patient needs to change, a two-person approach suggests strongly that the analyst be thinking about what needs to happen in the analytic relationship to facilitate the desired change. Ultimately, the goal remains the facilitation of intrapsychic change in the patient (See Schwaber, 1996), but the vehicle for that change is the therapeutic relationship in all its complexities. Altogether, Wallerstein's collected wisdom regarding the idiosyncratic nature of analysis and analysts supports the theory that there is no one analytic technique or body of theory.

Current formulations emphasizing the role of the relationship in the therapeutic action may threaten the intellectual primacy of psychoanalysis as a theory. But it helps explain why patients who participate in other types of treatment still manage to have a deep, positive therapy experience. Participation in the relationship is far more important than theorizing about it. Yet psychoanalysis potentially offers patients unique opportunities to understand themselves in that only psychoanalysis provides the awareness of the unconscious, of the need to repeat past patterns of behavior, of the primitive feelings that we all experience, even as adults. Essential to the analytic approach is the multiple sessions per week usually required to facilitate and work through a regression. This last point is extremely important in that regression is at the heart of the interpersonal analytic experience. Without some regression, there is no major breaking down of defenses, no access to primitive fears and wishes, and no joining together of analyst and patient at the most basic emotional level.

The original question, "What is the goal of psychoanalysis?" begins with awareness, insight, and the minimizing of distortions created by the transference. Clearly, each of these goals fits nicely in the intrapsychic classical definition of analysis. Yet, from my clinical experience, I have had better outcomes facilitating a more interpersonal analysis.

What ideally happens in an analytic treatment is that the patient forms an attachment, begins to reveal the transference, the analyst responds with a countertransference, conflict ensues, and each begins to feel misunderstood by the other. They may each feel a myriad of other things, such as unloved, unappreciated, abused, or taken advantage of, by the other. Or they may defend against these negative feelings by being madly in love with each other, or platonically idealizing each other. In any event, emotions run high, crescendoing into overt conflict and/or unbearable feelings of love and longing. Day-to-day conflicts, or "arguments," are common.

Traditional analysis required the analyst to "interpret" the true meaning of the patient's discontent with him. Relational analysis requires both parties to examine how and why they are in conflict—what led up to this event, how each person experiences it, how each person's history sets the stage for the current conflict, and, finally, how they must reveal their emotional responses to each other and resolve the conflict as best they can.

Typically, once the emotional air has been cleared, the *patient* makes his own interpretation, which is often deeper and always more meaningful than the analyst's interpretation. Some clinicians resist this definition of analysis, in spite of the fact that the concept of interpretation has been retained. Perhaps because it switches the most significant responsibility for interpretation from the analyst to the patient, the analyst may see himself as stripped of what he believes to be his most pivotal role in the treatment.

Two-person analysis, as I have defined it, changes the role and major responsibilities of the analyst, but certainly does not diminish his or her significance or degree of responsibility. The shift in role involves moving from interpreting observer to active participant and facilitator. The requirements for the analyst continue to include a deep knowledge of human experience and the struggle for transformation, but also demand a high degree of self-knowledge and openness to being affected and changed by patients. The analyst must be willing to be continually transformed by his or her therapy experiences—something that naturally is harder to do with maturity and experience.

The goals of the process I am describing are also different from the original goals of analysis as stated earlier. Relational analysis starts with this same goal, but goes beyond it. Patients who do well achieve not only a high level of self-awareness but also a high level of self-trust, so that the analyst is no longer needed to help mediate between the patient's wishes and fears, and reality. A more interpersonal approach, pioneered by the likes of Sullivan, Fromm, From-Reichmann and Levenson, is vital to achieving the goal of trusting one's intuition and experience, because feedback from the analyst is critical to the patient's acquisition of confidence in his own perceptions and gut reactions. The outcome of a more interpersonal analysis is therefore that *the patient learns about himself, not just in terms of increased consciousness, or early determinants, but also in terms of how he interacts with other people and the impact he has on them.* Through the medium of affective communication from the analyst, the patient learns by receiving the analyst's affective communications, registering them, and allowing them to alter his view of himself and the world. In this sense the transference is not only diminished, but can be altered in significant ways. At the conclusion of analysis the patient not only knows himself, but trusts himself, and is able to act constructively on what he knows to be true.

Finally, we need a context for considering theoretical contributions and effectively applying them to the clinical situation. Wallerstein (1992) notes that while there is an element of truth in every theoretical formulation, none is completely comprehensive and each follows a particular theme. How do we account for this?

Each theoretician perceives the world within the framework created by his or her own early experiences (a point made by many others, including Stolorow and Atwood). We are quick to analyze writers and poets based on their childhood experiences, as well as our patients. But we have been reluctant to shine the same light on ourselves. The simple truth about the incompleteness of any single theory, and the selectivity typical of any theoretician, is that each of us theorizes within the context of our own early experience, which includes the many societal influences that press on us. Though Freud's personal life has been put under the analytic microscope in recent years, from the questioning of the universal nature of the oedipal conflict to possible reasons for abandoning the seduction theory (Masson, 1984), living analysts are not subjected to such scrutiny.

When we do consider the personal motives for particular analytic theories or practices, this is typically done through the venue of gossip. Is it true that Freud slept with his sister-in-law? To what extent does the Oedipal theory describe Freud's childhood experiences rather than an inevitable developmental conflict? Did Kohut focus so heavily on the need for selfobjects because of his own narcissistic vulnerability? Did Greenson promote the "real relationship" based on his personal needs for friendship and affection from his patients? For instance, did he really help Marilyn Monroe on with her fur at the end of her sessions? What is the relationship between Socarides enduring commitment to the pathological etiology of homosexuality, with heavy emphasis on the ineffectual, weak father and domineering mother, and the fact that his own son has openly declared his homosexuality?

Rather than reserving our questioning for cocktail parties and critical biographies, we could gain more from accepting at the start that each person's psychological theory is inevitably influenced and determined by his early experience with family members, by the social norms and practices of the time, and by his own analysis. Forrester (1990) says that

"Analysts bring with them the fruit of their own transference to their own analysts."

So rather then gossiping about the early determinants of Jung's or Adler's or Freud's or Lacan's theories, I think we are ahead by *assuming* that what any one of us says about the human condition is, at best, true of ourselves and, at worst, a defense against what is true of ourselves. Additionally, anything that is true for me will be true for someone else, and may be equally untrue for others. The less idiosyncratic a person's life experience is, the more likely he is to generate universal ideas. The more idiosyncratic this experience, the more likely the theory is to have selective applicability and to achieve cult status rather than general acceptance. In any event, no single person has had such broad experience that he is able to theorize accurately about every aspect of human development. In this sense, Wallerstein's acceptance of pluralism is not only an expression of tolerance but one of inevitable truth. The existence of a single, all-encompassing theory is literally impossible because only an analytic Everyman or Everywoman could create it.

For example, my observations about the essential regression and merger aspects of deep relationships, including psychoanalysis, emerge from my own history of intense, shared experiences beginning with being born a twin. Twins tend to be very relationship-oriented individuals—for obvious reasons. So, does my status as a twin allow me a greater-than-average knowledge of relationships, or am I projecting my own early experiences onto the analytic situation? Also, I continue to be concerned with the role of countertransference, and the potential harm that can be done by *failing to disclose the countertransference*. Again, this perspective arises from my childhood empathic precocity and my parents' hesitancy to confirm my observations for fear of burdening me with their problems. My analyst did the same thing, and I fought hard to convince her that her unwillingness to acknowledge the correctness of my observations was countertherapeutic. As I write about the world as I have experienced it, I feel confident that I am addressing the truth. Reading the work of others who have come to similar realizations, such as Searles, helps strengthen my confidence. Yet at the same time, I know that there are other "truths" that I am missing because I have not encountered them in my life experience, or because the perspectives I currently have preclude my seeing and knowing these other truths. Rather than attempting to know things that I do not, I satisfy myself with the incompleteness of what I do know, and leave the rest to others.

Theory comes from practice and, ideally, affects practice. As such, it is inevitably idiosyncratic, multiplistic, and fluid. Deleuze (1977) describes the utilitarian quality of any good theory:

> A theory is exactly like a box of tools. . . . It must be useful. It must function. And not for itself. If no one uses it, beginning with the theoretician himself (who then ceases to be a theoretician), the theory is worthless or the moment is inappropriate. We don't revise theory, but construct new ones; we have no choice but to make others. It is strange that it was Proust, an author thought to be a pure intellectual, who said it so clearly: treat my book as a pair of glasses directed to the outside; if they don't suit you, find another pair; I leave it to you to find your own instrument [p. 208].

Looking at psychoanalysis through Deleuze's glasses requires us to be agents for change, not only in our consulting rooms, but in our theorizing. His perspective encourages us to indulge our uniqueness and even our idiosyncracies. Rather than implementing a theory or technique that we cannot relate to, perhaps our greater obligation is to "find another pair" of glasses that provides a clear and broader view of the world.

The material I present in the following pages thus represents my cumulative life experience, both in and out of the consulting room, and reflects my early relationships, sibling order, socioeconomic status, and the cultural forces at work in my generation. The ideas that I present are "truths" for me, and the techniques I advocate have worked quite well for me as a psychoanalytic practitioner. I trust that others have had similar experiences, and also different ones. As ecumenical as this may sound, I also believe that there are "right" and "wrong" ways of practicing, in that experience has taught me that certain approaches and behaviors by therapists are almost always destructive, such as boundary violations, defensiveness, nonresponsiveness, refusing to be forthcoming with a patient who is asking for your perceptions, etc. So, while we must each find our own way and our own voice, I don't believe that everything is relative or unique to a certain therapeutic dyad. Rather, we keep working to define a basic structure and approach to treatment that works, and we find our own voices within that structure and within the bounds of our responsibility to our patients. I present the ideas in this volume toward that end.

Chapter 1

On Seduction, Intellectualization, and the Bad Mother
Underlying Assumptions in Psychoanalysis

A fter almost a century of discussing psychoanalytic theory and practice, I am consistently amazed at the many aspects of the analytic enterprise that are rarely mentioned. Our reluctance to admit what we actually do and say when we are working with our patients remains the norm. Worse than that, however, is the tendency to *omit* the mention of interventions that might be controversial. That is, even when clinicians *are* talking about what they actually do, they frequently fail to include a behavior that they fear being censored for, such as, taking a patient's hand, or disclosing their feelings. The absence of honest discussions of technique has naturally created a most unfertile ground for innovations.

Another largely ignored aspect of psychoanalysis involves examining the premises or assumptions that underlie the whole analytic endeavor, both in theory and practice. It seems to me that it is difficult to propose revising something that is not adequately defined in the first place. The two-person paradigm evolved from an encyclopedic amount of evidence suggesting that we were overlooking important aspects of the analytic relationship. After decades of accumulating clinical data and experience, we could no longer deny that the analyst's individual personality had as much to do with what happened in the treatment as did the patient's. Yet this fact was strictly denied for many years, followed by a long period of slow recognition of the analyst's impact on the patient.

Thus, the two-person paradigm is not a new invention, but rather an extremely critical recognition of something that has always existed. If this sounds like a diminution of the two-person position, let me assure you it is not. The willingness to recognize the reality of the two-person paradigm is vitally important to the development of analytic technique. It is the difference between a flat world and a round one. Armed with this new perspective, we are in a position to develop the tremendous potential of the analytic relationship.

Although I continue to share much of my colleagues' excitement over the developments in the two-person perspective, it seems to me that progress in developing new theory and techniques remains painstakingly slow. We are still reluctant to talk about technique, and there is a regrettable resistance to changing what we do to accommodate our new paradigm. Somehow we want everything to be new, yet we also want everything to stay the same. People are willing to accept a relational model if it doesn't mean changing the way they do treatment. But if reconceptualizing the analytic relationship doesn't translate into technical changes, how important can these theoretical changes be? I don't think we can have it both ways.

Even though accepting the two-person model and redefining the analytic situation accordingly may seem like more than enough to focus on, I think there are many other realities waiting to be discovered. What else have we overlooked within the treatment situation? Are there not dozens of assumptions that determine our behavior at every turn, even though they may be more unconscious than conscious? Laplanche (1973) discusses our reluctance to scrap Freudian psychoanalysis and start over, retaining what seems to work and tossing what does not. "The Freudian system is never criticised, put in doubt; no-one ever envisages rebuilding it on surer foundations. New concepts are simply added each time a new difficulty is perceived" (p. 2). Rather than simply adding more new concepts, perhaps Laplanche is right and we need to further deconstruct psychoanalysis in order to build something better. In this chapter I will present some of the assumptions and characteristics of the analytic situation that I believe have been overlooked, or given inadequate attention. I discuss these aspects of theory and/or practice for the purposes of defining the reality of the analytic situation and to provide a foundation for the chapters that follow.

The Overvaluing of Intellectualization

One might argue that the over-intellectualization of any body of knowledge is inevitable. That is why Foucault argues against theories and labels. Simmel (1984) preceded him in noting that once a set of laws or rules have been set down they tend to be self-perpetuating, resulting in stagnation. I could argue, in fact, that in the act of writing about theory I am only contributing to the mass of intellectualization that stifles creative acts in psychoanalysis. And no doubt this is true. No matter how much I might emphasize that theory is nothing more than a tool, and that each person must find the right tool for the job, I run the risk of people interpreting my clinical guidelines as "rules" or taking my clinical observations as facts. (On the other side, of course, I also run the risk of being ignored altogether on the basis of presenting material that is alienating.)

So how are we to make observations, name those observations in some meaningful way, and then attempt to generalize those observations into legitimate broader categories without simultaneously creating obstacles to new experience? The answer is that we cannot. But there is much we can do to minimize the reifying effects of our attempts to organize what we know and share it with others. We accomplish this through dialogue with each other and through consistent interaction between theory and practice. Ultimately this leads to throwing out any theoretical concept that cannot be used clinically. Deleuze (1977) says,

No theory can develop without eventually encountering a wall, and practice is necessary for piercing this wall . . . a system of relays within a larger sphere, with a multiplicity of parts that are both theoretical and practical [p. 206].

Thought of this way, analytic theory and practice can join together to create a "living" entity, that is, one that is open-ended and sees change as vital to its continued relevance and existence rather than as a threat. Along the same lines, Orange (1995) encourages the concept of conversation increasing our "access to the whole" and of holding our theories "lightly" and in a "fallibilistic spirit." Although no one would argue with the idea that we need to work constantly to keep the lines of communication open, and to keep open minds, psychoanalysis is nonetheless known for its dogmatism.

In recent years there have been more attempts to maintain an open dialogue between divergent groups. Mitchell's innovation in the world of analytic writing, the creation of The Analytic Press's journal *Psychoanalytic Dialogues*, is a prime example of this concept in action. Subsequently adopted by other journals, the dialogue format presents different views simultaneously, stimulating the reader on multiple levels and precluding the passive acceptance, or rejection, of the work of a single person.

Over-intellectualization of the analytic process not only threatens us with stagnation, but also denies some of the basic realities of the analytic situation. For example, the early belief that interpretation was the chief instrument for facilitating the therapeutic process created a very narrow, and unworkable, prescription for clinical interventions. We have known for some time that most of what we do is *not* interpretation (Compton, 1975) and that the change process probably relies a great deal more on emotion than intellectualization. That is, the acquisition of insight depends on a unique emotional experience antecedent to that insight.

All of us know far too many people who have been "analyzed" for extensive periods and yet seem emotionally impermeable. They can rattle off their pathology with jargon-filled aplomb, and may even choose to discuss the intimate details of their personal history at dinner parties. What enables them to use their own painful experiences for the purposes of entertaining others or demonstrating their enviable degree of openness is really a perversion of the analytic ideal. They have achieved enormous intellectual insight without the benefit of emotional connection or integration. They represent the consummate caricature of psychoanalysis— the talking head. They can discuss what one would expect to be painful and feel no pain at all. It is as if they are talking about someone else. Chused (1996) addresses this same point.

All too many adult patients have gained intellectual understanding with little change in psychic structure or behavior, and many of the doubts about the therapeutic value of verbal interpretations and insight that have surfaced throughout the history of psychoanalysis are based on observation of these "interpretation resistant" patients [p. 1050].

Chused suggests that patients benefit more when they make their own interpretations, which is undoubtedly true. And she acknowledges that the patient makes these interpretations as the result of an emotional shift. In response to a moment of emotional dissonance, the patient necessarily creates a new experience to resolve the dissonance. Intellectual insight is the *naming* of this experience. Although a vitally important part of the process, intellectual awareness follows, rather than precedes, the emotional experience.

Most analysts would agree with the statement that emotional experience is at the heart of a good psychoanalysis. Yet most of what we talk about is intellectual, or intellectualized. The primacy of emotion in human experience, and therefore the analytic experience, has not been fully acknowledged and our techniques suffer accordingly. Orange (1995) says,

I think the failure of psychoanalysis to grant emotion a life of its own may account for the persistence of the widely accepted idea that we do not know how psychoanalysis heals. None of the official explanations provides an answer to why it works when it works, and why it does not when it does not [p. 98].

I agree with Orange that it is time to give the world of emotion its due. Certainly we can do so without fears of throwing out the valuable intellectually-based framework of analytic theory. Equally, we need not give up the acquisition of insight as a priority. Affect has recently become a popular topic in psychoanalysis, and deservedly so. But the step that we have yet to make is the one where we recognize that without intense affective experiences within the treatment, there is no deep and permanent change. More emphasis on facilitating affective experience, and the developing of responsible techniques for doing so, await the revolution in psychoanalysis.

Determining the importance of affect in the change process, and noting how the affective interplay between therapist and patient facilitates or hinders the analytic process, is a huge task. It is also a necessary one. For example, in my clinical experience I have observed that the patients who seem to change the most are those who are capable of deep grieving, that is, crying profusely or sobbing. Patients who achieve equal levels of insight without this profound affective experience do not change to the same degree. I have to admit that I do not understand why this might be true, yet I believe it is.

I also think that simple changes in the way we discuss cases, both orally and in the literature, could add greatly to our body of knowledge. For example, most clinicians do not say much about what they are feeling when giving a case example, unless they are specifically discussing countertransference. But now that we have accepted that our emotional responses to our patients are ongoing and unexceptional, I think we could learn a great deal by regularly including this information in our case discussions. As long as we continue to value what we think more than what we feel, we are in danger of excluding the information that is most important.

Mutual Seduction in Psychoanalysis

Another ignored aspect of the analytic situation is the mutual psychological seduction that occurs in every therapist-patient relationship. Friedman (1997) says that Freud did not so much design a form of treatment as he *discovered* one. And he defines the essence of Freud's discovery as the "power of psychological seduction." He says, "By seduction I mean an arrangement whereby the patient is led to expect love while the analyst, in Freud's words, plans to provide a substitute for it" (p. 26).

Friedman goes on to say that the analyst is deliberately ambiguous about how he feels about the patient, in hopes of avoiding the traumatic collision between the patient's fervent desire (to win the analyst) and the somewhat disappointing reality. Ideally, the patient experiences the rewards of the analytic endeavor and becomes so invested in this experience that he or she comes to tolerate the personal loss of the analyst as a love object. (Friedman does not address what the consequences are when the patient succeeds in becoming the analyst's love object.)

I agree with Friedman's assessment that Freud, and all of us who follow him in the work of psychoanalysis, are in the business of this seductive dance. And I also agree that Freud did not create this phenomenon. Rather, he seemed to deny the reality of mutual psychological seduction, claiming that the realm of seduction belonged only to the patient.

Gerson (1996) explains this as Freud's fear of his own desires, as well as reflecting the cultural values of the times. He offers an explanation of Freud's early admonitions to maintain a certain distance.

> These first usages make clear that the concepts of neutrality and abstinence were designed as technical guards against male desire and fear in relation to their experience of the female patient as dangerously seductive and that these concepts have their roots in the misogyny of the times [p. 629].

Thus we see Freud as a man who understood the power of what he had observed in his consulting room, but also as a man who feared the power that patients could have over him. He feared the results of acknowledging his own buried needs and desires. As he proceeded to define the psychoanalytic situation, he noted one truth (that the patient seeks to "psychologically seduce" the analyst) while denying another (that the analyst also seeks to seduce the patient). Having denied this need to seduce, he naturally was kept from enlightening analysts about managing the countertransference, which arises from this basic relational need.

Forrester (1990), in his book, *The Seductions of Psychoanalysis*, severely criticizes classical psychoanalysis for its seductive maneuvers. He sees it as encouraging docility, and unnecessarily infantalizing the patient and denying his or her real experience with the analyst. He sees sexual feelings as being particularly prone to denial. "The *indeterminacy* of knowing whether it is past seductions by the parents or present seductions by the analyst is what is interesting—because unspoken—when it comes to these skeletons in the closet" (p. 254).

Only recently have analysts felt freer to admit to their sexual feelings for patients. Yet we do not discuss the more generic need to "psychologically seduce" the patient as part of the analytic process. As a result, we cannot discuss the inevitable phases of approach and withdrawal, satisfaction and disappointment, victory and defeat, neurotic fears of rejection and grandiose visions of importance that each member of the analytic pair experiences.

For example, how much can, or should, we be aware of our own seductive maneuvers? Certainly some patients need to be 'seduced' more than others.

Diane, a thirty-something woman who socially is completely isolated, has depended on the "kindness of strangers" to meet her interpersonal needs. What I mean by this is that she has relied on the company of therapists for most of her social interaction. I am her third long-term therapist, and she has been in multiple session-per-week treatment for the past twelve years.

To say that Diane is phobic about intimacy is an understatement. The product of a broken home with a psychotic, highly intrusive mother and remote father, she has been severely depressed since her mother abandoned her forever when she was fourteen. I have been treating Diane for three years and am on the verge of despair. I have tried psychologically to seduce her for this entire period, and to some extent I have succeeded. I know I am very important to her, yet she does nothing to indicate that I am, other than whining uncontrollably and telling me I am selfish when I schedule any time off.

To say that I am running on fumes is to say the least. I have never treated anyone who gave me so little gratification. She has made *some* progress—she is less negative and argumentative at work, she exercises regularly, and she at least attempts to make some social contact with her peers. Intellectually I understand that she is terrified of being controlled (which she consciously knows and admits) and would rather be alone than lose herself to a crazy, intrusive person again. But emotionally, it is increasingly difficult to spend any time with her (I see her three times a week).

She hates being alone, has been preoccupied with the notion of suicide for years, and begs me to help her out of her prison. I see Diane as someone who cannot engage in the mutual psychological seduction that Friedman discusses. She cannot do it with me, or with anyone else. Therefore, she is alone.

In this scenario one might ask whether this person is treatable. Can someone ultimately be treated who cannot go through the basic steps of forming a relationship, of trying to win someone, and letting that person win you? My goal in treating Diane is to help her trust enough to be able to engage emotionally with me. She will not give me anything, both because her mother gave her so little, and because she is deathly afraid of the very engagement I am talking about.

Although Diane has no memories of being molested, she manifests many of the symptoms of someone who has been, including telling me that I should feel free to take advantage of her sexually at any time—that she would not resist. When I asked her why she thought I would want to do that, she said she didn't understand the question. It was as if she believed that anyone would want to molest another person if she knew she could get away with it. When I asked her why she would want me to do such a thing, she said, "At least I would be important to you in some way." Naturally one has to wonder what childhood experiences led up to these expectations. And it is rather easy to see that Diane sees masochistic submission as the path to a relationship, while she remains emotionally closed off and isolated.

In relational terms, is it possible to alter Diane's prototype for intimacy, that is, a situation where she is abused and withdraws deep inside herself, to a healthier scenario where she willingly attempts to engage and win the interest of another human being? I don't know the answer to that question right now, but I do feel sure that, in human terms, this is what needs to happen. (Obviously this is a very difficult and complex case that could be discussed endlessly in more clinical terms. But for the purposes of this illustration, I want to focus purely on the aspects of psychological engagement, or as Friedman says, "psychological seduction.")

The example of Diane brings us to the question of how much control over the mutual seduction is possible? Does someone like Diane need to be seduced more, because she offers little opportunity for interaction on her own—or less, because she equates opening up with annihilation? How much conscious control do we have over the mutual seduction process and how much, as in all relationships, is accomplished via unconscious-to-unconscious communication? Is this something we can have any control over, or only something we can observe once it has occurred?

Friedman, in the aforementioned paper, also says that the analyst avoids letting the patient know how much he really cares, or does not care, about him. In this way, the patient stays "on the hook" until he is in a position to appreciate what the analyst actually has to offer. But what about when the patient already knows, for example, when he has a sense that his analyst loves him, or hates him, or needs him? Forrester says it is part of the sadistic nature of the authoritarian seduction that denies the patient the affirmation of what he knows to be true. How much do we reveal to a patient who already knows the truth? When does a sincere attempt to be nonintrusive give way to "cat and mouse?" And when does a sincere desire to be forthcoming give way to unbearable levels of stimulated longing or desire?

Friedman seems to assume that the patient, who begins the relationship wanting the analyst as the love object and must settle for treatment instead, will not be successful in winning the analyst as a love object. The patient's defeat may be hypothetically desirable, yet we know from experience that this is not always the case. What happens when the patient *does* become the analyst's love object? Does this necessarily mean that all bets are off? (And when does eroticism reach a point where the treatment is no longer viable?)

Does this victory by the patient violate the necessary conditions for treatment, or is this only true when the analyst refuses to admit that she loves the patient? Little (1951) says that patients *do* become their analysts' love objects over time—that this is unavoidable. But the numerous cases of patients who have been sexually abused by their therapists, or who have been traumatized by being "dumped" once the analyst becomes aware of his or her feelings, indicate that the patient's victory in this arena is a mixed blessing at best.

Once again, we are left with more questions rather than more answers. But if we were to feel freer to discuss what makes a good "match," and to what extent we are consciously aware of our attempts to engage our patients (and be engaged by them), perhaps we could come to a better understanding of what makes for a "good seduction," and therefore a good basic treatment relationship.

For myself, I have made the decision not to treat anyone I do not like at first meeting. There has to be something that interests me about the person and makes me want to learn more about him or emotionally feel a pull to help him in some way. If this personal motivation is lacking, then I find a way to discourage the person from entering treatment with me. Because experience has taught me that it is as important for me to want to engage with him as it is for him to want to engage me. If I do not care about psychologically seducing a particular patient, then I am probably not the right therapist for him. He is better off searching for someone who does have this interest.

You might ask about the patients who seem inherently noxious, the ones whom nobody likes. Who will treat them if we all discriminate in the manner I am suggesting? I'm not sure that this presents a real problem. There always seems to be someone who shares just enough of each person's past experience to make a connection possible. So perhaps the criterion for a good match is simply, "I want to seduce (get inside) you and you want to seduce (get inside) me."

Does Analysis Exist Without the "Bad Mother"?

One of the most significant questions that I have asked myself in recent years is "Does psychoanalysis exist without the concept of the 'bad mother'?" (Or the bad object.) The classical position generally treats the "bad mother" as a creation of the frustrated child, who may or may not have cause in reality to find his or her caretaker to be deficient or abusive. Object relations theory takes frustration and disappointment in the parent-child relationship for granted, as do other two-person psychologies. It is part of the human condition.

Since early childhood experiences combine with genetic predispositions to form the adult patients who come to us, we naturally want to understand what they experienced during their formative years. I do not see this as a problem. The problem arises in our need not to be cast in the role of the "bad mother." Yet this is exactly what happens when the transference takes hold. We move from being the idealized, perfect parent or lover, to being the abandoner, rejector, or abuser. Goldberg (1992) notes the inevitablilty of a certain sequelae.

All analyses begin with enough shared understanding enjoyed by both participants, enough common ground to move on to the inevitable next phase; that of misunderstanding. From understanding—that is, a basic set of like-mindedness between persons—we move to misunderstanding—a breach of unity [p. 113].

I have spoken elsewhere (Maroda, 1991) of countertransference resistance that often accompanies the movement from understanding to misunderstanding. We like being idealized, provided it does not go too far. And we like being the benevolent one.

And once again we are faced with an inherent contradiction between our intellectual knowledge and our emotional responses. Intellectually speaking, most analysts would not disagree with the statement that we are bound to be the "bad mother" or "bad object" at certain times. Yet, in reality, we naturally resist this experience. Being cast in this role puts most analysts in immediate conflict. We see ourselves not as the disappointing or abusing parent, but rather as a good person who will not harm the patient. So we balk at the seemingly unfair accusations being cast our way.

Hirsch and Roth (1995), in their discussion of the interpersonalist tradition in psychoanalysis note that Sullivan believed he could remain outside the transference-countertransference mix. In contrast they note that

While most contemporary interpersonal analysts no longer view themselves as objective "experts," some do maintain that it is best to stay outside of the transference-countertransference matrix (Havens, 1976; Witenberg, 1987). These interpersonalists tend to believe that they can avoid being the bad or old objects. They posit that the analyst is able to provide corrective experience without first becoming lost in repetition of pathogenic internalization [p. 269].

Hirsch and Roth's observations bring us to the point that certain analysts, and therapists in general, believe they can escape becoming the bad object. It is the desire to escape this fate that is the basis for a strong belief in "corrective emotional experience."

There is no question that the game of bad-object hot potato is a dangerous one. If I, as the analyst, am not the bad object, and the patient needs to experience "someone" in that role, who else is left? Obviously, only the patient. That is why the safest possible situation for both patient and therapist is simply to stay outside the transference-countertransference interplay and let the real parents, spouse, boss, colleagues, etc. be the bad objects. But if we do this we avoid the reenactments that are necessary for real change. Levenson (1994) discusses the analyst's need to be seen as one who cares, which strikes me as being an aspect of the analyst's need to be the "good object."

> We must distinguish caring as a state of being, and *a priori* instrument of treatment, from caring as an emergent process between two people. Why am I caring? Because I am a caring person? Then you had better not threaten my perception of myself [p. 704].

The therapist's aversion to being the "bad object," as well as the patient's same aversion is a complex, multilayered event. I, as the analyst, do not want to be the bad object because I am still clinging to the belief that the pains of my life are someone else's fault. I think all of us, at some level, wish to remain innocent. If we did something wrong, it was an honest mistake. It was done out of ignorance, or naivete, rather than malice. Taking responsibility for our anger, hatred, sadism, envy, our desire to destroy both what we love and what we hate does not come easily. I think we are not much different than anyone else in this respect. Yet we have taken on the huge burden of representing ourselves as being capable of addressing reality, of knowing the truth. And we do not admit how overwhelmingly difficult this task is, and how much we are destined to fail.

Historically, we have been quick to note when our shameful feelings appear to have been stimulated by the patient. Although I believe that projective identification is a real phenomenon and, as such, a name for it is necessary, the term has become synonymous with patient-bashing. I am not the one who hates and rages, my patient is. Again, we have a tradition of making someone else the bad object.

To take this exploration even further, it might be true that we, as therapists, have not come to terms with our own parents' failures. When this is so, the patients' parents can become the "bad objects" not only in the patient's life, but in our own. I realized once when I was particularly angry at a patient's parents for being undermining and symbiotic that I was over-reacting and that this scenario was one that frequently upset me. It was only then that I realized how much easier it was for me to be angry at my patient's parents instead of being angry at my own. Concurrently, it was easier to be slightly contemptuous of my patient for not trying harder to break free than it was to be disgusted with myself for similar concessions.

The patient, of course, is engaged in the same mental gymnastics, trying to avert self-blame or trying to salvage a positive view of his own family. Very often severely abused patients cannot admit their parents' failings, in part, because of the old adage that "the apple does not fall far from the tree." To see that one's parents are sadistic, egocentric people is only one step away from seeing those characteristics in yourself.

One could argue that the entire psychoanalytic endeavor hinges on this assignation of responsibility for bad or evil things. And that psychoanalysts struggle to put themselves on the side of good. Initially, the analyst is blissfully idealized—a necessary first step for both parties. This honeymoon period allows for the mutual engagement and bonding between therapist and patient. And it provides a safe haven, albeit an illusory one, for the patient to explore his pain and sadness. Ultimately, however, this period must come to an end.

The patient knows he has internalized the "bad object," but cannot bear this reality. De-idealization of the analyst provides a segue from seeing the parents as bad to seeing himself as bad. Negative aspects of the analyst's personality and professional conduct provide a "not me" experience for the patient. The patient learns to forgive the analyst over time, as a model is built for accepting ambivalence and inadequacy. The analyst goes through a similar phase, moving from resenting or hating the patient for his criticisms and attacks, to forgiving him for these same behaviors. The therapeutic crescendo occurs when both analyst and patient achieve a reasonable degree of acceptance of their own "badness," weakness, lack of character, and inadequacy. Once this is done both parties are free to integrate these negative self-aspects with positive self-aspects, resulting in a more realistic and healthier self-image. Ferenczi, well ahead of his time, wrote about his observations that patients needed both his admission of weakness and his forgiveness. He made these notations in 1932 in his clinical diary, which was published later (1988).

> Sin
> Confession
> Forgiveness
> There must be punishment [Contrition, p. 215].

The chief obstacles to this therapeutic mutual hating and forgiving lay in both parties' resistance to seeing themselves as they are—and to seeing their parents as they are. Another form of resistance comes from the unrealistic goal that many patients unconsciously bring to their treatments. They seek psychoanalysis, as they would seek religion, in pursuit of redemption. At the heart of redemption is the desire to be released from the knowledge of evil, to be delivered from sin and restored to a state of innocence. In other words, they wish for the impossible. (Grotstein [1994, 1995] discusses related ideas regarding the need for sacrifice and "exorcism" in his writing on projective identification.)

The classical Freudian analyst understood the position of evil in relation to the patient. The patient in Freudian analysis needed to confront his primitive "evil" self. The problem with this configuration is that the same rules did not apply to the analyst. The analyst was somehow above or beyond this configuration. She was neither the bad parent nor the good one. She may have secretly felt superior but, through the medium of neutrality, did not assume any value-laden role. Hirsch and Roth (1995) note that many interpersonalists (and self-psychologists) try to define the role of therapist as "good parent," which may well constitute a tragic flaw.

They state that while those adhering to a developmental arrest model see that the "true self has been submerged or undeveloped" (p. 266). Somewhat mockingly, the authors present a view of treatment from the developmental arrest perspective:

The patient is relatively naive, resting in the arms of a wiser, parentified therapist. The therapist's attunement, holding and containing functions, empathy, optimal distance, and willingness to be used are the primary catalysts for the patient's growth [p. 266].

Hirsch and Roth see that neither the classical Freudian position nor the developmental arrest position posit a realistic view of either the unconscious or the analytic situation. They argue for a more balanced view that accounts for mixing it up in the transference-countertransference. I agree with the implication that neither patient nor therapist can be assigned the good or bad object roles on a consistent basis. We are constantly provoking each other to both positive and negative feelings, inspiring love, hatred or indifference.

The best way to negotiate this difficult terrain has yet to be determined. But I have consistently favored the use of self-disclosure when done at the patient's initiative (Maroda, 1991), and still see the use of this technique as vital to the working through of the transference-countertransference dynamics.

Creating new analytic techniques that address the complexities and emotional demands of a two-person psychology requires a new vision of the analyst as a person. It goes without saying that the ideal of the analyst as portrayed in training programs needs to change dramatically. And most analytic education would benefit greatly from focusing more on the inevitability and necessity of the analyst's exposure as imperfect and disappointing.

The role of personal analysis is also critical. If I have not deeply grieved my disappointments with my family, my spouse or partner, my analyst, and the realization of my own limitations, how can I keep from defending against this self-knowledge when I do therapy? If I have not mourned the losses in my life, including the de-idealization of the self, and the loss of innocence, then what do I have to offer?

Since this book seems to be a study of polarities, I might add, what if I have suffered too much, grieved *too* much? What do I have to offer then? Somehow the knowledge of what is heartbreaking and disappointing must be balanced with optimism and a faith in one's own desire to do good in the world.

What Does Mutuality Really Mean?

Aron (1996) notes that mutuality refers to any number of aspects of the analytic situation and does not preclude asymmetry. What is shared is not necessarily shared equally. More specifically, he provides a working definition of mutuality, distinguishing the relational position from the Freudian one.

> I believe that what may be the critical difference between most Freudian analysts and most relational analysts is that Freudians assume a relatively well-analyzed, relatively healthy analyst who can monitor intermittent countertransference disruptions through continual self-analysis. . . . Relational analysts, by contrast, assume, first, that in spite of having undergone an intensive analysis of his or her own, the analyst nevertheless is inevitably drawn into ongoing enactments with the patient [pp. 127–128].

Aron also provides a thorough literature review on mutuality and includes discussions of mutual regression, mutual recognition and regulation, and mutual intimacy. His description of the relational position leaves no doubt that the analyst and patient are partners in the treatment, albeit unequal ones.

But what does that really mean? How unequal are we, exactly? And how asymmetrical is the relationship supposed to be to maximize therapeutic benefits? I find that it is far easier to acknowledge intellectually the emotional co-involvement of therapist and patient than it is to implement this knowledge clinically. How do I behave differently once I have accepted that it is the transference-countertransference interplay that is to be analyzed rather than simply the patient? The stickiest problem revolves around analysis of the countertransference. How much time do we spend on the analyst's psychodynamics and how much on the patient's? There are a number of pertinent questions that need to be addressed, such as: How vulnerable do I want to make myself to a particular patient? How much access is the patient pushing for? What's the difference between mutuality and mutual analysis? What if I don't want to be analyzed at the moment? Do I have the same rights to decide when and how I want my participation to be analyzed, just as the patient ideally does?

Before we can attempt to answer these questions we have to recognize that both analyst and patient are essentially trying to do the same thing, namely, break down each other's defenses. We often speak of our own desire to break through the patient's defenses, but little notice is given to the mutual action by the patient. Over time, most analytic patients want desperately to know their analysts and may go to great lengths to break down our defenses. If one accepts the notion of mutuality in relationships, this is perfectly understandable and reasonable. Mutuality demands that the analyst show emotion and vulnerability to the patient at some time or another—preferably with some regularity. I think classical analysts often accomplished this through their body language, facial expressions, and voice intonations. For many patients today this subtlety of expression is not enough. They demand, and need, the articulation of feeling that their parents often withheld from them.

Mutual analysis differs from mutuality in that it allows the patient to analyze the analyst, relinquishing the notion of asymmetry. Ferenczi's (1932) courageous experiments led him to abandon mutual analysis as unworkable, in spite of the many things he learned about himself, his patient, and the process. He came to the conclusion that we do "not allow them to concern themselves with our person any more than is necessary for *their* analysis" (1988, p. 45).

If we speak of mutuality in the sense of mutual emotional giving over or surrender, the analyst need not do more than reveal his emotional reactions to the patient in the moment. Although patients often want more information, the heart of the therapeutic exchange lies in the mutual expression of deep feeling, and in the experience of shared vulnerability—not in the accumulation of personal information.

Prior to the acceptance of the two-person model, analysts felt free to have their own emotions, or lack thereof, independent of the patient. The acceptance of mutuality means that the analyst loses personal freedom and anonymity in the therapeutic situation. On one hand, this loss of freedom is one of the trade-offs for having any close relationship. On the other hand, I see the concept of mutuality easily becoming a demand on the analyst to feel what the patient feels—implying that the analyst is deficient or unempathic if he or she does not have this experience.

That is why the emphasis in my own work has been on emotional honesty rather than simply on mutuality. I often do not share my patients' feelings. Sometimes my patients claim to love me and I not only do not love them, I do not feel loved *by* them. At other times a patient has said nothing about how she feels about me, yet I am overcome by feelings of tender devotion. In my work on countertransference I have spoken of the frequency with which severely disturbed patients who demand love invariably stimulate anger or hatred. What is at work in these situations is the patient's inability to express his or her own hatred. Instead, these feelings are stimulated in the analyst and the analyst acts therapeutically by being able to recognize and constructively express the feelings of hatred that the patient has disavowed. The essence of mutuality lies in the analyst's co-participation and emotional honesty, not in the unequivocal sharing of the patient's experience. I find it unfortunate that so many people have interpreted mutuality primarily in terms of positive emotions, giving short shrift to the primitive and aggressive impulses. Although mutual respect, affection, and even admiration may facilitate an analytic treatment, it is the dark side of human nature that most often needs to be visited.

I think much would be lost if we lean toward a narrow, idealistic vision of mutuality that naively expects only the best of both people in the analysis. Although relational theories are often considered more egalitarian and respectful of the patient, this does not negate the reality of the presence of malice, sadism, and character flaws of all sorts in both analyst and patient. Greater equality in the treatment relationship necessarily levels the playing field; it does not necessarily elevate it.

Finally, I would like to add a note regarding the analyst's need for privacy. Although I advocate disclosure when the patient is actively seeking it, it is also true that sometimes we do not want to be known by the patient. Our need for privacy, or our lack of trust in a particular patient, may frustrate that person. Yet we need to have our own defenses at times, just as the patient does. We are not perpetually available emotionally and should not imply that we are. To do so only sets up another unrealistic analytic ideal that we must inevitably fail to meet.

Power, Control and the Role of Enactment

When I was a young graduate student I read the analytic literature in awe of the analyst's uncanny ability to understand absolutely everything about the patient and to execute precise maneuvers aimed at bringing the patient to self-awareness. I wondered if I could really be an analyst because I could not imagine myself ever being that omniscient and in control of the treatment situation. When I began practicing I continued to note a marked disparity between the tone of analytic case studies in the literature and the reality of my constant struggles as a clinician. As a young therapist I often felt confused and began to be aware that I felt in control of precious little, including being unable to control how I felt when I was with my patients. Equally, I was just as confused about what I should do next. Why wasn't I like the analysts who wrote in the journals? When would I acquire wisdom and uncompromising control? Armed with these questions, I entered my personal analysis, convinced that my analyst was perfectly healthy and in control and would pass these traits on to me.

As my analysis proceeded I learned a great deal about myself, about my analyst, and about the process. Not only was I not achieving perfection, I discovered I had a lot more problems than I thought I did. Even worse, I discovered that my analyst had a lot of problems, too. Not that she told me about them. She didn't. But as all patients do, I began to see her vulnerabilities, her failings, her conflicts. And when I confronted her with her own problems, I ran into massive resistance. She, too, believed that she was supposed to be healthier than I was and in control of what happened in our relationship. In order to maintain her self-esteem she had to believe she was more than what anyone could be. And I felt degraded and resentful about her implicit belief that she was healthier than I and always in a better position to evaluate what was happening between us. She had bought the analytic ideal.

In fairness to her, I was a difficult patient. I knew too much and wanted to know more. I was unrelenting. Sometimes I was demanding and intrusive. But she couldn't tell me to back off, which would have been emotionally honest. Instead, she thought she was supposed to be unendingly empathic. And that wasn't good for either one of us. I wanted and needed the truth. She wanted and needed to see herself as all-giving. When she had had enough of me, she would become cold and distant or give sadistic interpretations. Her resentment *had* to go somewhere. I asked her to be honest about her feelings, but she said that was not what she was supposed to do. Over time she relented in many situations, but did so with so much guilt that she often recanted her previous admission of emotion at our next meeting. The chaos of this situation was extremely stressful for both of us.

When my analysis was over I finally knew that I would never meet the analytic ideal. But I also understood that it was inhuman and unattainable. My personal analysis taught me that nothing good came from the pursuit of the impossible. My new goal became to learn as much as I could about what was really possible—to throw out much of what I had been taught, or what had been modeled in the literature, in favor of a real exploration of the analytic situation.

Like many of my colleagues I have come to the conclusion that enactment is inevitable (see chapter 6). Not only is it inevitable, it is what distinguishes psychoanalytic treatment from other more behavioral or supportive approaches. Psychoanalysis is unique in its pursuit of the past for the purposes of working through in the present. Other non-analytic therapies may end up inadvertently doing the same thing, but only analysis has reenactment as a goal. Classical analysis implicitly stated that the patient recreates these past scenarios, *not in reality but in his mind. Reenactment was relegated to the world of fantasy.* Although I do not deny the role of distortion, displacement and denial in the therapeutic process, it seems to be true that the patient recreates the *emotional scenario* that existed in the past.

For example, my patient, Susan, comes from a very unnurturing, militaristic family background where she was taught self-reliance to the extreme. Her parents were not demonstrative and did not allow any independent thoughts or actions. Any disagreement was treated as insubordination and dealt with harshly. She was the first born and, to the dismay of her younger siblings, would endure all manner of verbal and physical punishments rather than give in to the parents' demands. As a result she and her parents had an increasingly combative, disruptive relationship that crescendoed predictably during her adolescence. Her parents then arranged for her to go to a good boarding school, purportedly to advance her beyond the limits of the small town in which they lived.

When she told me about boarding school she expressed guilt over not really enjoying it after her parents had gone to great trouble and expense. A couple of years into the treatment she had lunch with a longtime family friend. While discussing her childhood, the family friend casually remarked on the decision to send Susan to boarding school as inevitable because "I think your parents just didn't know what else to do with you." My patient reported this remark to me with some confusion. It had never consciously occurred to her that her parents had sent her away to school primarily to get rid of her.

I can easily say that my relationship with Susan is the most combative one I have ever had with any patient. We disagree and engage in power struggles frequently. She says she doesn't want it to be this way. I concur. Yet the "fighting" goes on. (I discuss this patient throughout this book and give a detailed description of our struggle over physical contact in chapter 7). At one point, in response to Susan's criticism and laments that I was not meeting her needs, I became so exhausted and disgusted I told her that perhaps she should seek out another therapist who might satisfy her. A couple of sessions later she became very agitated and confronted me. She said, "You want to get rid of me, don't you? You're sick of having to deal with me and you don't want to have to bother any more. You'd be relieved if I left, wouldn't you?" I replied with something like, "Yes, I *would* be relieved. *And,* I wouldn't. There's no question I am very ambivalent about you and about continuing this treatment. Yet I am committed to finishing it and know that you need to finish what we've started." She was very upset about my feelings, yet calmed down for the first time in weeks—once I admitted that I might be relieved if she left.

My scenario with her was a reenactment of parental ambivalence and a desire to be rid of Susan. It may have directly been a reenactment of her banishment to boarding school, or a condensation of repeated instances when she felt her parents wished her gone. I did my part of the reenactment by actually feeling ambivalent about treating Susan, yet I behaved differently than her parents in that I admitted my negative feelings toward her rather than acting them out by ending the treatment.

When I first practiced psychoanalysis I thought someone like Susan was supposed to *imagine* that I wanted to get rid of her when I really did not. Then I would interpret this so-called fantasy to her, she would realize its accuracy, and she would relive her grief and rage from the past. But often that is not how it actually works. What really happens, at least in my experience, is that the enactment is frequently inevitable. It must be alive in the present. I must actually reach a point where I want to get rid of Susan as much as her mother did, and I have to be able to admit that. Then, and only then, can Susan express her grief and rage. We repeat the past emotionally, but not factually. And we are typically aiming for a much different outcome.

Analysis is more of an emotional event than an intellectual one, not only for the patient, but also for the analyst. It is the recreating, expressing, and working through of emotions, by both analyst and patient, that constitutes the therapeutic action of psychoanalysis. And though we might like to believe that it is always the patient's past that is recreated, I have made the point elsewhere (Maroda, 1991) that often the analyst's past is recreated and enacted as well.

I always tell my patients that they cannot control what they feel—only what they do. And this principle can be equally applied to us. Beginning a treatment with the knowledge that almost any emotional experience is possible, and uncontrollable, leaves analysts in a better position to accept their feelings, no matter how primitive or abhorrent, and to be in control of their behavior.

What Is the Agent of Change in the Analytic Process?

Traditionally, change was thought to occur when the patient developed a "transference," felt the emotions inherent in the transference situation, and developed insight regarding the nature and origin of these feelings. Making the unconscious conscious. The analyst remained neutral, but not inactive. The analyst was not a real part of the emotional event, which took place in the patient's mind and necessarily involved a distortion of the here-and-now relationship with the analyst. The analyst's skills came into play through astutely picking up on the meaning of a phrase, or intuiting the patient's unexpressed emotional state. Giving accurate interpretations and observations helped the patient to feel known, accepted, and able to delve further into his own psyche. The metaphor of the classical analyst at work has often been the archeologist—digging for buried treasure in the depths of the unconscious, moving slowly and carefully from one level to another so as not to inadvertently damage or bury a precious find.

Strachey's (1934) classic article on the nature of therapeutic action remains the definitive statement on this topic, which points to both the critical nature of Strachey's comments and also to the subsequent avoidance of this topic in the analytic literature. Since we do not really know how analysis works, and because analysis has already been assaulted incessantly for proclamations involving untestable hypotheses, there seems to be a marked tendency *not* to venture out on the limb of how analysis works.

Recent articles tend toward recapitulating what has already been said, rather than proposing anything new. Meissner (1989) revisited Strachey, giving this generation a summary of the classic paper and emphasizing its seminal nature. These include Strachey's emphasis on the motivational power of transference and the qualities of the quintessential therapeutic moment, the "mutative interpretation."

> Strachey identifies several qualities of such mutative interpretations. First, they must be emotionally immediate or, as he says, "directed to the point of urgency." He explains: "at any given moment some particular id-impulse will be in activity; *this* is the impulse that is susceptible of mutative interpretation at that time, and no other one" [p. 142].

Strachey's notion of the "point of urgency" is an important one. We all intuitively understand what he means by this phrase, because we have experienced these moments in our clinical work. Yet it is also true that the "point of urgency" is almost always identified after it has occurred. It is a retrospective observation given on the heels of a successful intervention. It is difficult to deliberately facilitate these moments because we cannot usually identify the "point of urgency," either before it occurs or even while it is occurring. When what we say or do collides in an atom-smashing way with the patient's defenses, the result is a period of calm introspection and mutual relief.

As stated earlier in this chapter, Chused (1996) speaks of the therapeutic moment as an "informative experience," which she says is followed by the patient's own interpretation and occurs when the analyst *refrains from participating in an enactment* (emphasis mine). I agree with her basic notion of change, but disagree with her stand on enactment. She says that "informative experiences create the emotional dissonance between expectation and experience needed for a shift in perceptual frame, so that what we once denied or ignored is now seen" (p. 1051). Chused's position on what is therapeutic coincides with Strachey's—both emphasizing that the analyst provides a therapeutic moment by behaving differently than the patient's early caretakers.

> If all goes well, the patient's ego will become aware of the contrast between the aggressive character of his feelings and the real nature of the analyst, who does not behave like the patient's "good" or "bad" archaic objects. The patient, that is to say, will become aware of a distinction between his archaic phantasy object and the real external object [p. 369].

Strachey emphasizes how important it is not to be the "good" or "bad" object in reality, because this does not allow for the patient to have the analyst be whatever he needs him to be. (So much for corrective emotional experience.)

The views of the therapeutic action of psychoanalysis presented by Strachey and Chused can be labeled "classical," in that they rely on relative anonymity by the analyst, and revolve around a moment of truth when the patient sees that his view of the analyst represents a distortion rather than the truth.

Loewald's (1960) classic paper reiterates this same notion, but adds the concepts of integration, internalization, and formation of new, more positive object-relationship with the analyst. Loewald sees the analyst as representing a higher level of organization which provides a therapeutic model that is eventually internalized by the patient.

Modern notions of mutuality, relationality, intersubjectivity, and particularly social construction, add on or depart from this traditional view of the therapeutic action of analysis. Gehrie (1996), in his review of Kohut's perceptions of what is therapeutic, quotes him as saying, "'The gradual acquisition of empathic contact with mature selfobjects is the essence of the psychoanalytic cure'" (p. 189). Kohut's view could easily be seen as an extension of, or compatible with, Loewald—yet adds much greater emphasis on the critical nature of relationships.

Mitchell (1988) reviews the classical and developmental arrest models of therapeutic action, with particular attention to the work of Winnicott, noting his emphasis on returning to early infantile states and allowing the

patient to use the relationship with the analyst as a corrective environment. Mitchell sums up the classical position and developmental-arrest
position, and goes on to define the relational-conflict model.

> The classical position places the analyst outside the analysand's
> relational matrix, pointing his finger at its archaic and conflictual
> workings and enjoining the patient to renounce its doomed infan-
> tile promises. The developmental-arrest position also places the
> analyst outside the analysand's relational matrix, luring the patient
> away from its constrictions and offering something better. The third
> perspective portrays the analyst as discovering himself *within* the
> structures and strictures of the repetitive configurations of the
> analysand's relational matrix. The struggle to find his way out, the
> collaborative effort of analyst and analysand to observe and under-
> stand these configurations and to discover other channels through
> which to engage each other, is the crucible of analytic change
> [p. 292].

I share Mitchell's acknowledgment that there is something to be said for
all of these views, each containing some inherent truth about the analytic
process. Since the goal of this chapter is to point out what might be true
about analysis in practice, yet is not articulated in theory, what might I
add to this discussion of the therapeutic action of analysis?

First of all, I would like to comment further on some of the views I
have presented here. I agree with the conventional assessment of Strachey's paper as brilliant. And I both agree and disagree with what he had
to say. I agree with his notion of "point of urgency"—essentially a window
of opportunity for a therapeutic intervention. I favor replacing the term
"mutative interpretation" with "mutative intervention," which allows for
the full repertoire of therapeutic action. Strachey says that

> mutative interpretations usually take place within the transference.
> Extratransference interpretations are less likely to impact on the
> point of urgency, since the impulses tend to be distant in time and
> space and thus lack immediate energy [p. 143].

Strachey's advice presaged the discoveries of cognitive theory and
behaviorism. Immediacy has proven to be critical to behavioral change.

I also think that the point of urgency can be seen as a moment of heightened affect in the transference and that this is a critical variable for change. Thus, "immediacy" combined with "emotion" equals "point of urgency" or, if you prefer, "point of change."

As stated previously, Strachey believed that the analyst's lack of aggression toward the patient would be curative as the patient became aware of this fact. Similarly to Loewald's conceptualization, the analyst would become the new and improved, less aggressive introject. And I do not dispute that this can, and does, occur. But it is certainly not an all-inclusive explanation for change. (And, again, it points to the analyst's need to deny his or her own aggression and potential for being the bad object.) What about when the patient is extremely provocative and the analyst *is* very angry? Even when the analyst attempts to hide his anger, even his "interpretations" ultimately reveal his true feelings. Cooper (1997) has noted that interpretations such as "I think you are trying to make me angry" or "Is there some reason you would want me to be angry with you?" are thinly-disguised personal statements of the analyst's anger. They are, in effect, de facto self-disclosures. So if the patient takes in that the analyst is angry, perhaps *very* angry, how is this moment therapeutic?

Returning to the notion of immediacy and emotion equaling opportunity for change or transformation, then there is no reason why *any* emotion could not potentially be therapeutic, including intense anger. Loewald's point about aggression is well made in the sense that a consistently sadistic analyst will certainly fail to be very therapeutic toward his patients. But if we can, for the moment, assume that most analysts are reasonably capable of feeling and behaving constructively towards their patients, then the honest acceptance of the patient's emotion, and/or the honest expression of emotion *toward* the patient are all potentially therapeutic.

The old warnings about being either the "good" object or the "bad" object certainly have merit in that the analysis is doomed if the analyst, or the patient, are determined to cast each other into one of these roles exclusively. If we take emotional honesty as the only authentic therapeutic stance, rather than the unachievable neutrality, then no emotions are off-limits or inappropriate for either person to feel. What is often ignored in analysis, even in discussions of the "good enough" analyst, is that we are not necessarily better or worse human beings than our patients' caretakers were.

What we have to offer our patients is not a superior presence, but rather an opportunity to help them be aware, accept, express, understand and integrate their ambivalent emotions. And as Mitchell says, the venue for this therapeutic action is not the individual, but the relationship. The two-person paradigm offers an opportunity to make the most of this relationship, with the analyst's emotional honesty serving, in part, to facilitate the patient's.

We are currently trying to understand better how the relationship serves as the vehicle for therapeutic action in psychoanalysis, and most of this book is devoted to exploring some of these complexities. In summary, the core understated aspects of this therapeutic action involve mutual emotional honesty, mutual emotional availability, and an atmosphere of mutual trust. How the relationship works as the vehicle for change is the topic of the remainder of this book.

What Is the Goal of Psychoanalysis?

The goal of making the unconscious conscious, or "where id was, ego shall be," are obviously far too simplistic as the outcomes of psychoanalysis. In recent years we have learned that the transference is never obliterated, only subdued and managed (Schlessinger and Robbins, 1983). We have also learned that patients who maintain their improvements over time have acquired the ability to soothe themselves in times of need (Schlessinger and Robbins, 1975). As more outcome research appears, we can use this knowledge to inform both our goals and our techniques. The more we learn, however, the more evident it becomes that awareness, and even structural change brought about through integration, are not enough. Ideally, the patient who has completed an analysis has a reasonable awareness of his emotional life, understands how his history and biology converged to create the person he is, is reasonably able to manage his emotions, and can both love and work.

Criteria for all of these functions vary, of course, depending on where the person started, and what resources he or she brought to the analysis. Most of the above concepts are relative ones, yet are measurable in some way. Can the person sustain a relationship, regardless of how imperfect or perfect it may be? Can the person hold a job, regardless of whether the work is a great passion or minimally interesting? Can the person bear what he or she is feeling without drugging it away, splitting it off, or dumping it onto someone else? Analysts don't often speak in such mundane ways about outcomes, perhaps because our original goals were so unrealistically lofty.

Yet there is much to be said for these basic behavioral measures of treatment success, regardless of modality. And modest achievements remain achievements, nonetheless. Even Strachey, writing during the time when most people thought analysis could actually "cure" people, said this about the process: "It is, of course, a matter of common experience among analysts that it is possible with certain patients to continue indefinitely giving interpretations without producing any apparent effect whatever" (p. 375). We might add to his comments that it is possible to try all manner of interventions without necessarily producing any therapeutic effect. Thankfully, this is not usually the case. But I think that having smaller, yet meaningful, goals for analysis that incorporate the essential tools for living are critical to positive treatment outcomes.

Naturally, we also need to have larger goals that may not be measurable in the moment, but that fulfill some type of analytic ideal. Insight is difficult to measure, yet we know it when we see it. The same may be said for affective tolerance and integration, the capacity for empathy, or for that matter, the ability to love. The character of love is knowable on an intuitive level, yet impossible to gauge or define with any certainty.

So if we look at the "big picture" and attempt to create an overarching goal for psychoanalysis, what would that be? My answer to this question is born out of my own personal analysis, and the most successful cases I have treated. Patients ask me how analysis will change them, if all goes well. Will they be released from the depression that has haunted them their whole lives? Can they rid themselves of self-doubt, negative thinking, or wanting approval? I always say no. I tell them that their basic personality will not change. I tell them that no matter how much better they get, under duress, the old fears, bad habits, and negative attitudes will return.

But I also explain the value of self-awareness, insight and integration. I tell them they can be much better off than they are now through a series of small, yet extremely meaningful, modifications. I tell them it is all a matter of degree, and that the difference between being suicidal and not being suicidal, between having some idea of why you are experiencing a particular emotion versus being completely in the dark, between being able to resolve conflicts with co-workers versus getting fired repeatedly—that these cumulative changes can make for an entirely different life without having to create an entirely different person.

Most of all, I tell my patients that the goal of analysis is for them to know themselves and trust their own intuition and experience. I find that most pathology ends up being expressed through denying one's own perceptions, needs, and feelings. Getting better, regardless of diagnosis, centers on helping patients to listen to their gut reactions and learn to follow them in a constructive way. The notion of constructive expression of emotion depends also on a realistic view of the consequences of behavior. For example, a person who is quick to fall in love or develop infatuations and other impulsive idealized attachments may feel a strong desire to act on those feelings whenever they occur. While this may work out at times, it can equally be disastrous and surely threatens the individual's ability to remain in a committed relationship over time. Thus the realization of deep feelings of attraction and desire must be balanced with an equally deep appreciation of the potentially painful consequences of acting on those feelings. As Schafer (1970) said in his classic paper on visions of reality,

> What can one expect in this world? Are people and relationships with them different from, and perhaps, more than, one has been ready to realize? What can one expect of oneself as a person of a specific sort in this world? What are the costs and dangers of gratification; the consequences of error and protest; the prospects for success and failure, reward and punishment, pleasure and pain? ... [p. 279].

Any notion of trusting one's intuition and feelings must rest on this balance between internal and external reality. I can honestly say that I have never treated anyone who did not know the "truth" about themselves and the people closest to them, no matter what mental gymnastics they might go through to deny or split off that truth.

For example, Ethel, a middle-aged woman with a diagnosis of border-line personality disorder who had an 18-year history of treatment, including annual hospitalizations, never learned to manage her rage and feared that she would destroy others with it. Over the years that I treated her I began to see a pattern emerging that accounted for her "breakdowns." Invariably, she would start to "go crazy" whenever someone close to her was undermining or betraying her. During the time I treated her she was in a very passionate love affair, having left her husband for this other person. Over time she came to "know" that her lover was cheating on her. She would come to her sessions in an agitated state and make frequent references to her lover spending a lot of time with "so and so." Subsequent sessions revealed more agitation and mention of something like the lover taking a business trip with "so and so." Finally, I mentioned to Ethel that she seemed increasingly agitated and appeared to be concerned that her lover was cheating on her with "so and so." Ethel's response was to vehemently deny that she thought any such thing. She was merely noting a few random facts about her lover's recent where-abouts and meant nothing of the kind. How could I even imagine that her ideal lover could ever cheat on her? I answered by noting how upset she had been lately and how preoccupied she seemed to be with her lover's whereabouts. She told me I was "too Freudian" and should relax and stop over-interpreting every little thing.

Over the next few weeks Ethel followed her pre-hospital pattern of agitated depression that led to spending days in bed without bathing and to drug and alcohol abuse. Finally, she was completely decompensated, behaving bizarrely, and had to be hospitalized. Years later, after her relationship with her lover had ended, she was told by a mutual friend that this lover had cheated on her repeatedly, and with the several "so and so's" she had mentioned to me in her sessions.

Ethel knew exactly what was going on, but could not admit it. She would go crazy at times like this because she could not manage the pain of betrayal and her murderous rage toward anyone who would treat her this way. Ethel finally stopped this series of hospitalizations when she learned to recognize and accept both the failings of others, her own failings, and the extent of her rage. The giving up of the idealized, perfect self, achieved through union with the idealized, perfect other, was critical to her aquisition of self-awareness, trust, and acceptance. Ethel achieved her sanity through eliminating these obstacles to knowing and accepting both internal and external reality.

I would like to explore this topic further through a less severe example. Amy is a 30-year-old married woman whose husband ushered her into treatment by calling me and making an appointment for the two of them. Once they were in my office it was clear that Amy's husband had only come with her because she would not have come on her own. Even though she was suffering from severe depression, had gained 40 pounds in two years, had frequent crying jags, and often would spend whole days in bed, this woman had not seriously considered seeking treatment. Her husband was very upset and concerned, and finally acted on her behalf.

Not surprisingly, Amy's depression and accompanying feelings of self-hatred were not new. She had attempted suicide in adolescence, but had done better when she left home and went to college. She moved even further away to attend graduate school, where she met and married her husband. For the first few years of their marriage they lived far away from Amy's parents and saw them only once a year. Amy was reasonably happy during this time and had no severe symptoms. Two years ago they returned to Amy's home town and have had constant contact with her family. During this time, her severe symptoms have returned, in spite of the fact that this move was Amy's idea.

When I asked Amy about her childhood she described a very lonely one, where her workaholic parents were constantly absent, building their fortune in their own business. As they grew more successful, they were at home less and less, but supplied Amy with money and a good private education. Not having come from money, and having worked very hard to achieve their success, they told her how lucky she was to have such a comfortable life.

But Amy didn't feel lucky. She felt neglected and sometimes abused. Amy's older brother had significant anti-social tendencies and regularly would physically and psychologically abuse her. She recalls leaving school and sitting in the park for hours to avoid this fearful situation. In the winter she was forced to go home and often had to lock herself in the bathroom to protect herself. She said the neighbors called the police once when they heard her screaming. I asked the obvious question: Didn't she tell her parents about this? She said she did, but they didn't want to hear about it. Her mother, who dominated the household, told Amy that she was burdening her after a long day at work and told Amy to simply stay away from her brother.

Likewise, whenever Amy was sick or crying about anything, her mother would tell she was "oversensitive" and should get a grip. Over time Amy came to the conclusion that her misery was completely her own fault. She accepted her mother's judgment that she was oversensitive, should not have the feelings that she did, and should have been able to tolerate her brother's abuse.

She told me her parents were highly regarded in the community, very successful, had overcome severe hardships from their own childhoods, and the only conclusion for Amy to draw was that she was both wrong and inadequate. She didn't think treatment would help because there was nothing to be done about her faulty character. Amy contents herself with being considered a nice person, being very pleasant and accomodating to everyone she meets. She is intelligent, personable, and attractive and prides herself on being able to get along with anyone.

Although there is no question that at one level Amy has accepted her mother's version of reality, and truly hates and doubts herself, she also knows the truth. When she told me of her brother's abuse and her failed attempts to escape him, I asked her if she really believed that being hit, verbally abused, and having her head stuck in the toilet were things she shouldn't be upset about? Would she feel this way if someone else told this story? She quickly admitted that abuse like this was intolerable. The only possible reason for "blaming the victim" would be if that person were provoking the abuse. She said quite earnestly that she had not provoked her brother beyond the normal sibling squabbling, and added that her brother had a history of beating up other children and torturing animals without provocation. (Even though he was the aggressor, the brother obviously needed help as much or more than Amy, who was even-tempered and approval-seeking.)

"So you don't really believe that you deserved or provoked the abuse by your brother?" I said.

"No, not really," said Amy.

"And you don't really believe that being constantly fearful, insecure, and feeling abandoned by your parents were unnatural reactions to your situation, do you?"

"No," she said. But she added quickly that somehow this must all still be her fault. When I asked why this was so, Amy was lost for an adequate answer other than that her mother had always made her feel this way, so it must be true. Down deep, Amy knows the truth but cannot trust her own experience because her mother not only did not validate Amy's feelings, but told her repeatedly that her feelings were wrong and unacceptable. More poignantly, Amy cannot admit the truth because she still desperately wants her mother's love and approval. With a mother who defines love as masochistic submission, and who rejects Amy for any independent thoughts, actions, and feelings, there is little hope of Amy having both herself and her mother's devotion. For now she has denied herself in pursuit of her mother. Since this cannot possibly succeed, she must eventually face the painful relinquishment of her mother.

My job is to help Amy find the voice within herself that knows the truth, to act appropriately on those truths, and to acquire a sense of trust so that she can listen to this voice and know what to do after she has left me. My view is similar to Modell's (1994) view of the private self which he differentiates from Winnicott.

> Winnicott observed a true self, a source of creativity and psychic aliveness that is dissociated from a false self, which acts as a buffer between the true self and the outside world. I prefer the term "private self," as it underlines the dissociation betweeen a social or public self that is known only to the individual and that is at risk of exposure. As far as I know Kohut did not describe such a private self. This difference in the conception of the self in turn leads to different therapeutic aims. My own concepton of the self is closer to Winnicott's in that I view the aim of treatment as facilitating a reconnection with this inner core of the private self rather than replacing that which is missing or deficient [pp. 208–209].

I agree with Modell and Winnicott in that I do not believe that the analyst facilitates the emergence of the true self primarily through a corrective emotional exprience. And I would go further in my statements regarding the goals of analysis. Emergence of the true or private self is not sufficient. Consolidation and acceptance of that self, the ability to trust one's own experience on a day-to-day basis (trusting your own intuition), along with affect management and the ability to express oneself constructively in the world—these are the goals of analysis. Once the private self emerges, the patient has to learn how to live with these suppressed (as in Amy) or repressed (as in Ethel) aspects of their own experience. Trusting their personal reality and then knowing how to negotiate with external reality are essential to functioning independently of the analyst.

The analyst facilitates this outcome through his or her emotional honesty, including the honest expression of hatred, anger, frustration, and envy. The patient does not need to be reparented in the sense of being loved and nurtured (it has taken me years to learn to love some of my patients) but rather needs the analyst to facilitate an experience of mutual emotional honesty, encouraging the patient to trust her own experience. As Levenson (1990) says, "The patient's vision of life is full of inattentions, repressions, distortions because that constricted vision is necessary to survival, by not mobilizing the anxiety of the person's caretakers" (p. 300). The goal of analysis surely is to remove these impediments to the patient's vision, or personal reality.

Facilitating the uncovering of the patient's emotional truth is not at odds with the fact that someone else might have another version of the truth. I am not teaching Amy that her truth is the only one. In fact, when she has expressed confusion and a need to know why her mother behaves the way she does, I try to help her understand that her mother lives in a completely different emotional world than Amy does. The more Amy understands her mother, and appreciates the differences between them, the better she deals with her.

What I try to teach Amy is that what she feels, thinks and needs is important. She already understands too well that what others feel, need, and think is important. I tell her she will not be happy with herself until she learns to respect her own experience and lives honestly, even if other people don't always agree with her or like her. As long as she has the same respect for other people, then she is not likely to go seriously wrong very often.

Encouraging Amy to know and trust her feelings, and to be assertive, may or may not sound very analytic. And it is not always so easily done. Often we spend days trying to tease out how she really experiences some situations. And analytic listening, observing, interpreting, and personally responding, are all part of the emotional education of Amy.

Amy's acceptance of what she feels inevitably leads to deep grieving over what she has denied for so many years. As she allows herself to experience her deep sense of loss—loss of a secure childhood, loss of her own feelings, loss of her parents' time and affection, loss of the acceptance and approval she still strives for—you can almost see how she is coming into focus. She is relaxed rather than painfully self-conscious, she is full of feeling instead of superficially friendly, her eyes are focused and deep instead of darting and slightly glazed, her body settles into the couch. Amy is finding herself.

Though this scenario appears to be quite blissfully successful as an analytic experience, there is another reality. Even though I feel that I am easily able to facilitate Amy's experience of herself at this point in the treatment, this will not always be true. For now Amy is quite non-threatening to me. She is pleasant, responsive, appreciative, and tenderly emotional. She is devoted to me and thinks I am wonderful. I care deeply for her and take pleasure in helping her to find herself.

One day, however, it will be me who is standing in the way of Amy's reality. One day I will be the object of her frustration, pain, and rage. Already she has begun to complain that the weekends are too long, that she feels abandoned by me. But she protests weakly at this point, still fearing that I will be like her mother if she shows too much feeling. And one day I will be like her mother. I will be having a bad day, or I will be feeling guilty about her pain and anguish, or I will be caught up in my own emotional world and will fail to be empathic toward her. I will defend against her and repeat the sins of her mother. And she will hate me.

Ideally these lapses will be occasional, yet they will be ongoing. They will be therapeutic because Amy will see that I am not perfect and that she does not need to be either. But in spite of my romantic desire to see everything as potentially therapeutic, there is no doubt in my mind that I will stifle certain aspects of Amy's personality without meaning to. I will be blind to what she needs in some ways. I will not be able to bear certain feelings beyond a particular point. I will not know things about her that I do not want to know about myself. I will fail her. Not in a subjective way, but in a real way. The only consolation is that everyone is destined to fail her in some way, and I have faith that I will do much more to help her than to harm her.

Conclusion

Psychoanalysis has always been an over-intellectualized process, in theory if not always in action, a point made earlier by the likes of Rank, Ferenczi, and Fenichel, to name a few. Analytic theory has neglected the emotional realities of both analyst and patient, tending to idealize what occurs in the mind. Many of the actual relational dynamics between therapist and patient are often overlooked in the interests of maintaining either the ideal of psychoanalysis or the ideal of the analyst. Although I agree with Schwaber (1996) that analysis is ultimately an intrapsychic event because the patient comes with exactly that goal in mind—to achieve some internal change that will allow him to leave and maintain himself independent of the analyst.

In the following chapters I illustrate the paradoxical nature of the treatment relationship, that intrapsychic change occurs primarily through interpersonal means, and that the vehicle for change is the emotional engagement that occurs between analyst and patient. The better we understand the nature of that relationship, the better prepared we will be to facilitate it.

Chapter 2

On the
Analyst's Fear of Surrender
Can Sex Be Far
Behind?

The notion of mutuality in analytic treatment has produced a new way of defining the relationship between analyst and patient. As we continue to color in the figure of the participant-analyst, as opposed to the observer-analyst, our own vulnerability and emotional state become more important to the analytic endeavor.

Many have spoken of the patient's natural desire to have legitimate power in the analytic setting (Little, 1951; Tauber, 1954; Greenson, 1971; Searles, 1973, 1975, 1979; Lomas, 1987; Hoffman, 1983, 1991, 1994; Maroda, 1991). Perhaps nothing is more critical to this sense of self-efficacy than the patient's desire to know that he has had an emotional impact on his therapist. As we conceive of the analytic relationship as one of reciprocal mutual influence, we realize that many of our patients wish to know us, penetrate us, and transform us to the same degree that they wish to be known, be penetrated, and be transformed. (This is not to say that they do not equally fear the same.) Or, as Aron (1996) stated previously,

> The patient and the analyst each want to be known and to hide, and each also wants to know the other and to avoid knowledge of the other. Both the patient and the analyst are motivated toward isolation and toward relationship, toward autonomy and toward mutuality, toward agency and toward communion [pp. 234–235].

Traditional analysis taught us to resist obvious efforts by patients to derail us from neutrality and abstinence, stating that the patient was attempting to defeat the therapist and destroy the treatment.

We fended off the attempts by our patients to influence us, move us, and have us acknowledge their impact on us, believing that we were being asked to recreate a pathological scenario that would ruin the treatment. Instead, we observed their efforts and forged our interpretations from this metal. But decades of experience have taught us the limitations of interpretation. And generations of new patients, produced by a less authoritarian society, have scorned our approach as cold and unresponsive.

As a result, our resistance to being influenced by our patients has been seriously questioned in many quarters. The flourishing literature on mutuality, self-disclosure, countertransference, and reciprocity have produced new ideas that threaten not only the primacy, but the validity, of the neutral or abstinent analyst. Cautions against being seduced into the patient's pathological re-creations have been replaced with even-handed discussions of role-responsiveness (Sandler, 1976), the patient's re-creation of past relationships out of the desire for relatedness (Mitchell, 1988), the inevitable mutual social construction of the analytic relationship (Hoffman, 1991, 1992), the productive use of countertransference enactments (Renik, 1993), and the natural desire for both analyst and patient to be alternately known and unknown (Aron, 1996). Mandates against acting out have been replaced with calls for responsible self-disclosure (Ehrenberg, 1992, 1995; Renik, 1995; Aron, 1991, 1996; Maroda, 1991, 1995a). These changes in psychoanalysis are not so much a result of changes in the patient population as they are changes in our perceptions of our patients' motivations, and subsequent alterations in our perceptions of what is therapeutic.

Equally vital to defining the new psychoanalysis is a reminder of the importance of maintaining the boundaries and exercising appropriate control over the analytic situation. Discussions abound regarding the nature of the "legitimate power and authority" of the analyst (Brenner, Kernberg, and McLaughlin, 1996), something I discuss in greater detail later in this volume. While we may not be able to claim that we always know best, we have not lost sight of the fact that we do know *something* and, last but not least, we can be held accountable in a court of law for what we do.

This leaves us with the questions: what exactly are we trying to accomplish; how do we facilitate this process within a mutual relationship; and, if being more human and emotionally available is really essential to our task, how do we accomplish this without unseemly gratification?

Although we do not have definitive answers to these questions, we are embarking on a new age of psychoanalysis that will lead us to greater understanding of analysis as a relationship. We are actively looking at the patient's need to influence the analyst, a topic closely associated with the patient's need for the analyst to surrender emotionally. For example, Hoffman (1994) comments about the patient's need to experience the analyst's emotional involvement: "When the patient senses that the analyst, in becoming more personally expressive and involved, is departing from an internalized convention of some kind, the patient has reason to *feel recognized* in a special way" (p. 189).

I think the therapeutic effect that Hoffman describes is related to the notion of surrender. Of particular interest to me is that the patient must *perceive* that the analyst has given over in order to achieve the therapeutic benefit. And this accounts for much of the frustration that we feel from time to time with difficult patients. Even though *how* we feel is critically important, it has minimal therapeutic impact if it is not *communicated* to the patient in a form he can understand. The more defended the patient is, the more overt the communication needs to be. While a moist eye might be more than enough for one patient, only openly crying would communicate the same level of empathy or sadness to another patient. And if the patient cannot bear to receive any emotional input from the analyst at a given point in time, he will need to flee or punish the analyst for violating him.

Searles (1978–79) was one of the first analysts to note how important it was for the patient to know that he was having an emotional impact on the analyst. He says,

> For the analyst to reveal, always in a controlled way, his own feelings toward the patient would thus do away with what is often the source of our patients' strongest resistance: the need to force the analyst to admit that the patient is having an emotional effect on him [p. 183].

I would add that this desire to know that one is having an emotional impact is a mutual one. Analysts' discussing their troublesome cases are likely to note that they feel frustrated—that no matter what they do they are not having an impact. Patients who are unhappy with their treatments say similar things. Clearly, whether we have talked about it in the past or not, both analysts and patients need to know that they are having a significant emotional impact on each other. Even when talking about the patient's experience, the notion of surrender appears infrequently in the literature. We are more likely to discuss the breaking down of defenses, which is an aspect of surrender, and avoid the broader and deeper issue of emotional "giving over" occurring as part of the therapeutic process.

To be effected by taken over

The Patient's Emotional Surrender

give up self

Ghent (1990) took a major step toward delineating the patient's experience of giving over in his now classic article. He defines the patient's emotional surrender as transformational, "the obverse of resistance" (p. 110), conveying "a quality of liberation and expansion of the self as a corollary to the letting down of defensive barriers" (p. 108). He describes the patient as having a buried longing for the experience of surrender, because the process of surrender involves letting go of the *false self*, implicitly allowing the *true self* (Winnicott, 1960) to emerge. While Ghent's definition relates to what is often called the "developmental arrest" model, I think that it can be applied equally to the notion of breaking through archaic defenses for the purpose of facilitating insight

to be effected — to let oneself be effected in
surrender + integrity of self   awareness

and emotional reintegration. Whether or not you are partial to the term "surrender," most analysts would not argue with the notion that giving up one's defenses leads to a certain emotional giving over within the relationship. One of my patients described it as "swinging out into space and letting go of the rope."

Although the literature on the topic of surrender, either unilateral or mutual, may be almost nonexistent, the process certainly is not. Patients and their analysts have been regressing together and surrendering to each other since analysis began, simply because this naturally occurs in a deep, unfolding relationship. It may also be fair to say that patients and their analysts have both been sabotaging the process of mutual regression and surrender with equal or greater frequency, out of their mutual fear of vulnerability, engulfment, penetration, and annihilation.

Khan (1972) goes so far as to say that the phenomenon of malignant regression, characterized by aggressive, negative therapeutic reactions, and/or excessive clinging constitutes a resistance to the process of surrender. (Khan lays the groundwork here for viewing benign or therapeutic levels of regression as the first step toward emotional surrender.) In discussing Balint's definition of malignant regression he says,

> The first proposition I wish to offer for consideration is that all the features that Balint so succinctly itemizes as characteristic of malignant regression are basically *reactive* in nature. They are an attempt to avoid and evade something else that a patient dreads and is threatened by from within: namely *surrender to resourceless dependence in the analytic situation* [p. 225].

Khan states further that these patients have split-off their aggressive tendencies and cannot reconcile them with attachment. Thus surrender represents an annihilation of the self, a loss of all necessary aggressive strivings for independence and self-definition. He illustrates his point by providing a touching case history of a young woman who desperately needed to surrender and who also lived in horror of losing herself to this process. Although Khan presents a cautionary tale with regard to the patient's emotional surrender, noting how difficult and combative his patient was, he does not present this case as an example of when surrender should be avoided. Rather he lets us know that some patients are so ambivalent about therapeutic surrender, so terrified of facing their own dependence and aggression, that they literally go kicking and screaming into this process. This takes quite a toll on the therapist as well as the patient.

Along the same lines, Hidas (1981) emphasizes the important therapeutic aspects of surrender, yet also says that "a psychological surrender may not automatically produce instant transcendence, but could be the door to various levels of darkness and purgation" (p. 29).

Both Khan and Hidas present a description of emotional surrender that I consider realistic. It is not a euphoric, unconflicted, calm spiritual experience—even in the healthiest of patients. Surrender occurs only after a lengthy struggle to maintain one's defenses. It is essentially what is "resisted" by both analyst and patient.

Bollas (1986), intuitively grasping his patients' desire for merger and subsequent surrender and transformation, attempted to explore the precedents for this behavior in childhood. He describes the mother-infant relationship, noting that the "mother continually *transforms* the infant's internal and external environment." As a result, he says,

> the mother is not yet identified as an object but is experienced as a process of transformation, and this feature remains in the trace of this object-seeking in adult life, where I believe the object is sought for its function as signifier of the process of transformation of being. Thus, in adult life, the quest is not to possess the object; it is sought in order to surrender to it as a process that alters the self [p. 84].

I think this last sentence of Bollas's is critical: "*surrender . . . as a process that alters the self.*" Based on my own clinical experience, I would take this one step further and state that surrender is *the* self-altering process. In the moment that a person surrenders he or she is irrevocably changed. In the psychoanalytic situation the "object" is, of course, the analyst, and the "process" is psychoanalysis. The patient surrenders through the medium of the emotional merger with the analyst and their shared regression. But the surrender itself is not to the person of the analyst, but rather a giving over to the patient's own emotional experience—losing herself to herself—within the containing framework of the analytic setting.

Ghent (1990) says, "The process is what is important; the object to whom one surrenders is irrelevant" (p. 112). I think this carries the point a bit too far, in that most patients cannot and do not surrender to simply anyone. Nor do they surrender in an atmosphere where it is feared or unwelcome. The medium for the transformational experience is the analytic relationship, and the analyst must therefore be skilled enough, and present enough, to facilitate the patient's surrender.

Surrender is seen as therapeutic and desirable by both Bollas and Ghent, but is defined as a process the patient experiences, not the analyst. This seems particularly odd to me coming from Bollas, who describes the need for surrender and transformation as universal and ongoing. As such, how is this need not applicable to the working analyst? Bollas (1987) also speaks of the patient's need for mutual regression, stating that some patients need to make the analyst "go somewhat mad," so that the patient can "believe in his analysis and *know that the analyst has been where he has been and has survived and emerged intact*" (p. 254).

How exactly do we communicate to the patient that we have shared his or her emotional experience and "emerged intact"? Many would say that our ability to be understanding and compassionate when the patient is in the throes of some overwhelming emotional experience is the best we can do. We seem to be more than a bit in love with Bion's notion of "containing" the patient's experience. Although there is no doubt that the therapeutic value of the containing function is very real, and something we have all experienced in our daily clinical work, I think this concept has been overextended, in part perhaps, because it reinforces the ideal of the analyst as calm, in control, and above the fray.

But certainly our patients do not always want or need us to be calm and unemotional. In the past many patients relied on their own intuition and reading of their analyst's non-verbal behavior and voice inflections to satisfy their need to access the analyst's emotions. Ask anyone who was analyzed at least ten years ago and they will probably tell you that they were expert at noticing the slightest variation in their analyst's voice, or style of dress, and grew to know what those variations meant. Yet many of our patients do not trust their own judgments and experience. Rather, they actively seek affirmation for what they consciously or unconsciously know about their analysts. And with fewer patients coming four and five times per week, they have less opportunity to become expert silent interpreters of their analysts' experience. Therefore the tide is shifting toward the analyst openly expressing emotion, thereby facilitating the patient's healthy pursuits of confirming reality and experiencing shared affect. Rather than frustrating our patients under the assumption that they intend to lead us astray, we now consider seriously that they may instead be leading us in the right direction.

However, in the pursuit of a more mutual relationship—one that will provide the needed degree of safety and active participation—the patient does to us what we do to him. That is, the patient actively works to break down our defenses. I think this is the single most important reason why we have needed to see our patients as wanting to defeat us: because they do want to break us down. What we failed to realize in the past is that this mutual aspect of the relationship is critical to the analytic endeavor.

Patients do not regress and surrender on their own. It is up to us whether we fight them in this process or whether we willingly participate. However, the same rules apply to us that apply to our patients. We do not give over easily; we usually do not give over to people we perceive as dangerous; we give over as part of a long-term relationship that builds through a mutual give and take; and we cannot give over if we feel threatened in some way—even if this has no rational basis. Mutual surrender is a relational achievement, not a given. It is the culmination of the working through of the transference-countertransference, and often follows a storm or conflict between analyst and patient. It does not come easily to either person, and can only occur with experience and mutual trust.

Yet we resist the experience of mutual surrender—for a variety of reasons. First, because we were taught to resist, based on the aforementioned erroneous beliefs regarding the patients' intentions. Second, because regression and surrender take up too much energy and concentration. (Winnicott said he could only regress with one or two patients at a time. The others had to queue up and wait their turn.) Third, we fear facing our own primitive selves that are revealed when our patients break through to us. Our feelings of empathic pain, lust, rage, envy, disgust, and love may sometimes be too much for us to bear. Fourth, we fear being hurt, rejected and/or abandoned in our moment of greatest vulnerability—just as our patients do. And fifth, we fear the sense of losing control emotionally—equating it with losing control of our behavior and of the boundaries. We fear forsaking our responsibilities to our patients in the pursuit of our own healing and gratification. Little (1951) said, "The very real fear of being flooded with feeling of any kind, rage, anxiety, love, etc., in relation to one's patient and of being passive to it and at its mercy, leads to an unconscious avoidance or denial" (p. 38).

Little refers to this as us being phobic about our own feelings—something that is often true of our patients. Ironically, we seem to share our patients' frequent perspective that admitting and expressing their true feelings will lead to disastrous behaviors, such as if they confess their murderous rage they might actually murder someone, if they confess their sexual feelings, they would have to act on them, etc. While I realize that we are only human and boundary violations cannot be eliminated, I do believe that more boundary violations result from the analyst's emotional dishonesty than anything else. It is not the feelings of lust or rage that lead to acting out, as Little says, but rather the *denial* of deep feelings and vulnerabilities that leads to acting out.

Gabbard's article (1996), "Lessons to Be Learned from the Study of Sexual Boundary Violations," concluded that most therapists who commit sexual boundary violations are not sexual predators, but are rather like the rest of us. He says,

> Many have felt that they were in love with their patients, others have self-destructively surrendered to demands for demonstrations of caring, and still others have been desperately needy and situationally vulnerable because of impoverished personal lives or acute stressors like divorce or death of a loved one. Perhaps most striking is that the majority of the therapists I have seen have had no previous history of ethical misconduct and are often even highly respected and prominent members of the profession [p. 312].

So it is the needy analyst that is most at risk. Yet all of us fall into this category at some time or another. And personal treatment does not serve as an inoculation. Gabbard says, "No evidence supports the idea that those with extensive personal treatment are less likely to engage in sexual misconduct than those who do not have such treatment" (p. 319).

What *is* characteristic of those committing boundary violations is that they frequently give in to their patients' demands for expressions of caring, illustrating Ghent's differentiation between masochistic submission (which he labels a "perversion of the wish for surrender," p. 119) versus true emotional surrender. Gabbard says these therapists tend to ignore their own needs and vulnerabilities. They offer self-disclosure and/or physical contact randomly, rather than at specific moments when the patient is seeking it. And their disclosures tend to incorporate much personal information rather than centering on an affective response to the patient in the here-and-now. They are also secretive about what is going on in the treatment situation when discussing the case with others.

Thus it would seem that mutual emotional surrender, which involves respecting and expressing the analyst's feelings as well as the patient's, is *not* what leads to boundary violations. Rather it is the denial of strong feelings and vulnerabilities, the inappropriate disclosure of personal information, and the masochistic submission to the patient's demands that lead to boundary violations. This can be restated as, "the therapist's *resistance* to the experience of surrender results in perversions of surrender, for example, pacification, masochistic submission, sadism, inappropriate self-disclosure, and/or sexual boundary violations."

Mutual surrender is *not* the same as mutual analysis. Mutual analysis, as mentioned in chapter one, emanated both from Ferenczi's sincere desire to break the impasse in his treatment of a very difficult patient, code-named RN, and was also the result of his masochistic submission to her. When Ferenczi was emotionally honest with her, he achieved good results. When he gave in to her demands to have him on the couch, the treatment was unworkable. Ferenczi learned much from this experience and later reported that his overindulgence of RN resulted from his resistance to knowing and expressing his countertransference hate toward this difficult patient (Maroda, 1998).

Mutual surrender is not an expression of the analyst's love, though the analyst may love her patient very much. Ferenczi taught us that expressing anger and hatred can be very therapeutic. Rather, mutual surrender constitutes an emotional opening up, a falling away of the analyst's resistance to being known by the patient in the deepest way possible.

As such, the analyst's surrender is both an intrapsychic and an interpersonal event. That is why analysts who do not self-disclose have been able in the past to communicate their *internal* experience of surrender to their patients through their voice intonations, body language, and word choice. But, as I said earlier, many patients need more. This does not mean that the analyst should randomly express whatever deep feelings she is having. I want to place the notion of surrender within the context of my technical recommendations on expressing the countertransference, that is, that it occurs at the patient's behest, is done only when the analyst can express herself constructively, and focuses primarily on emotion rather than information. Surrender and transformation occur within an emotional matrix, not an intellectual one.

Sometimes personal information may be necessary to create a meaningful context for the patient's understanding of the analyst's experience, but ideally this information would be kept to a minimum and only revealed as part of the analyst's emotional disclosure. Although I have always emphasized the importance of affect over information, I understand that sometimes it is impossible to communicate emotionally without some historical or anecdotal information.

However, my own clinical experience with self-revelation has taught me that patients can very quickly begin to wonder if you are reversing roles with them. So I try to keep it brief, particularly if I have not disclosed very much to the patient in the past. Patients vary tremendously in this respect, some having a great desire for knowing their analysts, literally bathing in the mutuality and deeply appreciating the analyst's willingness to make herself vulnerable; while other patients become uncomfortable and anxious if the analyst goes beyond the most parsimonious revelation. Like everything else, this has to be negotiated within each unique analytic relationship.

I would like to return to the case of Susan, whom I described in the last chapter. As you may recall, she suffered a painful childhood, marked by her parents' need for total control. They ran the household like a bootcamp, demanding complete obedience from their four children. Any infraction was punished quickly and severely. Susan was the oldest child and the only one who would not give in to her parents' demands for apologies if she believed them to be unreasonable or wrong. As a result, she was emotionally and physically abused, hit by both parents and thrown into the basement until she would apologize. This resulted in her occasionally spending the night sleeping on damp, dirty laundry.

She recalls these experiences as her parents' attempts to "break her." And she takes great pride in stating that they were never successful in doing this. You will not be surprised to hear that in the first few years of treatment she could not cry with me, and was intensely ambivalent about my facilitating deep feelings in her. Like Khan's patient, she desperately wanted to feel deeply with me, and would consider the session a waste if this did not occur. Conversely, she also became so fearful she would decompensate on the couch rather than cry.

Khan's notion of the "dread of surrender to resourceless dependence" fit this patient perfectly. Whenever she came close to giving over, she would mount an aggressive attack on me, making demands for longer sessions, reduced fees, love, and physical contact. As Khan said, her malignant regression resulted from her intense annihilation fears.

In my dealings with Susan I have observed her quest both for my emotional surrender and my masochistic submission to her. In a case like this one, where the patient actively seeks both types of giving over, it is easy to confuse the two. For example, Susan consistently tells me that she needs to hear how I am feeling toward her. She describes her mother as being a "wall," defeating Susan's attempts to take a "read" on her. She says that she remains frustrated to this day by her mother's emotional unavailability, and needs to know that she can have an impact on me—that I will be emotionally honest with her.

Susan's need to know how I am feeling toward her seems reasonable enough. Yet, in practice, it is far more difficult than you might think. She often comes to her sessions agitated on the inside, but highly defensive on the outside. She has even asked me to let her know when I observe her doing this. But even when I try to intercede, Susan often cannot let me in. Instead she will ask me what I am feeling. Sometimes I respond by noting that she often asks me to "go first." Other times I just try to respond. Often I end up saying that I don't really have any significant emotional response to her—that her feelings are on the inside and are not stimulating a strong response in me. She tends to feel thwarted by these responses, and becomes angry if I do not have an emotional response for her. Occasionally she comes to her session overcome with some feeling and we are able to communicate. But most of the time the sessions are a struggle for the two of us to connect with each other.

Early in the treatment Susan asked for things she needed, and complained about my therapeutic demeanor and techniques. She noted that the couch was too deep for her and that there should be back pillows for shorter patients. She also said the room was often too cool for her, and that there should be a blanket. After her repeated complaints, I went out and bought a cotton throw and pillows to put on the couch, which pleased her very much. She was now much more comfortable. (Note how this fits with Bollas's comments on the mother's early identification, not as object, but as transformer of internal and external reality. Traumatized, regressed patients often seem to require both physical and emotional adaptations from the analyst.)

She also asked to have the lighting dimmed when she had a late afternoon or evening session. She thought the lights in the office were too bright. She then requested that I move my chair closer to the couch, as I was too far away. In the beginning I didn't have too much of a problem with these requests. But later I noticed that Susan would become enraged if she came into my office and I had failed to dim the lights; or if I failed to move my chair closer to the couch. She became angry and accused me of wanting to hurt her and keep her at a distance. I noted that she seemed to want the responsibility for our closeness to be mine, rather than a shared effort. I told her to feel free to turn off the light next to her whenever she wanted to, or to let me know if I seemed too far away. But she refused to do this. "If I really cared about her, I would automatically do these things. After all, it's not like I don't know what she wants." Here we can see how the very same issue (Susan's physical comfort) can at one time be the focal point for both genuine desires to feel close and comfortable and, at another time, be the focal point for attempting to get me to masochistically submit. Which is why no single issue or incident can ever be confidently labeled as being this or that. It is not the subject matter that determines the nature of a communication between analyst and patient, it is the immediate emotional reality that exists.

It doesn't occur to Susan that my office setup is fine for me and all my other patients—that all of these requests are peculiar to her, and therefore difficult for me to remember. It also does not occur to Susan that I might develop resentment about having to be perfect in my responses to her wishes, or suffer the consequences of her rage and disapproval.

Over the past few years I have worked at forging a relationship with Susan that is more mutual. I give on things like the pillow and blanket, because I know she is genuinely uncomfortable. Without the pillow behind her back, her feet would not touch the floor as she sits on the couch, which she finds demeaning. She is genuinely cold in my office because I do keep it on the cool side and she is both very thin and very tense, which means that she does get uncomfortably cold at times. She wants to know that both her emotional and physical comfort are important to me, since neither of these mattered to her parents.

What I do not tolerate is being emotionally beat up because I have not moved my chair close enough. I let Susan know that I do not appreciate her way of telling me that she fears I do not want to be close to her. "Find another way," I tell her. To let her beat me up whenever she feels like it is not surrender, as Ghent says, it is masochistic submission.

As much as Susan struggles with letting go, she also desperately wants to do this. She tells me she cannot bear the physical pressure she feels when she needs to cry and cannot. She goes home from her sessions and paces like a caged animal. Yet when she arrives in my office, she closes up. Every time I pursue her feelings with some success, and she starts to give over, she begins to fight. She tells me she does not want to be broken. I tell her I am not trying to break her. She is not giving over to me, she is giving over to herself, to her own emotions. Intellectually she understands; emotionally she does not.

For better or worse, most of our closest moments have come when I am angry with her. When she is criticizing me nonstop or beating me up about something, I let her know I am angry, and do so with emotion. Then we have a heated exchange that provides a genuine emotional release for both of us. We agree at the end that it would be good if the same thing could happen with tender feelings, with sadness, even with pain. But aggression is safer and easier. And, oddly enough, in the heat of the moment we often do lose ourselves, momentarily giving over to feelings of sadness, relief, empathy, and even laughter. Somehow when we both get emotional enough (as long as I am not out of control), a window opens up between us that I would call surrender.

At these times we both feel depleted, exhausted, and emotionally spent. But neither of us feels beat up or violated. Whatever happened between us, no matter how difficult, was mutual. We reached each other, and understood each other as human beings in a way we did not before. A couple of times this has happened when Susan is sad, and she has looked and seen a moisture in my eyes. And I know she has seen it and I do not try to hide it. Ideally, as the treatment progresses, Susan and I will meet each other like this without so much aggression. We will be able to give over to each other no matter what each of us might be feeling.

The Analyst's Resistance to Surrender

Oftentimes we feel defeated when a patient breaks through our defenses, stimulating what can be an overwhelming flow of emotion and sense of vulnerability. Too often we feel that somehow the patient has "won"—implying that we have lost. Ghent (1990) notes that these feelings may be based on our cultural attitudes. He says "In the West surrender has meant 'defeat.' In the East it has meant transcendence, liberation" (p. 111). He goes on to say,

> In the East, to quote Heinrich Zimmer (1954), "the primary concern—in striking contrast to the interest of modern philosophers of the West—has always been, not information, but transformation, a radical changing of man's nature and . . . a renovation of his understanding both of the outer world and of his own existence." Perhaps we see vestiges of this distinction in the schism between analysts whose emphasis is informational (insight is what cures) as against those for whom the focus is transformational (with cure comes insight) [pp. 111–112].

I think this last statement is a profound one, and delineates the opposing camps in the world of psychoanalysis. Perhaps, regardless of the diversity within groups, psychoanalysis is rapidly differentiating along the lines Ghent has laid out: those analysts whose emphasis is informational as opposed to those whose emphasis is *trans*formational. Another way of describing the two camps is those who believe in the power of the mind versus those who believe in the power of felt emotion.

I place myself in the latter category, believing that "with cure comes insight," acknowledging that "cure" is an outdated and relative concept. However, I believe there is an emotional experience that necessarily precedes both the acquisition of genuine insight and the intellectual organizing of that experience. As I stated earlier, the point of change occurs at the point of emotional surrender. Although the objective of the analysis is the patient's emotional surrender, some degree of surrender on the part of the analyst is necessary to facilitate this process. Surrender qualifies as one of many relational events that is mutual, but not necessarily symmetrical. Even patients like Susan, who wish for complete mutuality, grudgingly accept over time that the analytic process must be asymmetric or no one would be in charge.

If we take a moment to remind ourselves of what we were looking for when we began our own personal analyses, I think few of us would deny that we were seeking transformation. Equally undeniable is that those moments of epiphany, if they occurred at all, did so during occasions of deep, personal connection not only with our own buried emotions, but also with our analysts.

Fears of losing control in the analytic situation have remained an obstacle to what I consider to be the most therapeutic moments in analysis. Informed by research on boundary violations, we now know that it is the resistance to deep feeling that is more likely to produce a boundary violation, rather than the willingness to lose oneself emotionally. Being lost momentarily and giving over to deep, even primitive, feelings, does not have to translate into losing control of the therapeutic situation. On the contrary, an analyst who is not afraid to surrender to her own and her patients' strong emotions, is more likely to transform them both.

Chapter 3

Show Some Emotion
Completing the Cycle of Affective Communication

The last chapter dealt with the issue of mutual surrender as a sine qua non for therapeutic action, that is, change. But what actually takes place in this moment of surrender that allows for change or transformation? In order to understand and facilitate a therapeutic surrender, we need to understand better the nature of affects and the role of emotion in individual growth and development, as well as in the therapeutic process. What follows is both a review of the relevant literature on emotions, and an application of this information to the therapeutic process. It appears that many, if not most, of our patients suffer from impairments in affective experience and regulation, and that there is evidence that we need to express our own emotions to facilitate our patients' affective development. Building on Stern's (1985) notions of *interaffectivity* and *affective attunement,* I propose that the analyst's affective responses are critical for completing the cycle of affective communication. This chapter concludes with an in-depth discussion of the clinical implications of the uses of emotion in analytic treatment.

Psychoanalysis and Affective Theory

First, what is the role of affect in classical analysis? Shapiro and Emde (1991) make the point that Freud and his followers "did not develop a coherent model accounting for affectivity in clinical theory and even less so in metapsychology" (p. iii). Blum (1991) adds that Freud focused rather narrowly on the notion of affective abreaction, or the notion of reliving a traumatic incident and catharting the disturbing emotions. (See Spezzano, 1993, for a comprehensive review of the literature on affect in psychoanalysis.) Little was known during Freud's lifetime about affective development, let alone the neurological foundation and locations for affective experience. I make this point not in the interest of criticizing classical theory or practice, but rather to emphasize the obvious: as research in human development and neuropsychology provide new information that has important implications for the therapeutic process, we have the opportunity to modify our ideas and interventions accordingly. And the topic of affect now affords us just such an opportunity.

The cumulative research over the past 30 years tells us much about affect development and the importance of affective communication. The essence of this chapter is that the *mutually affective moment* constitutes what is therapeutic between analytic therapist and patient. And that the therapist plays a critical role in helping patients compensate for early deficits in the ability to know, feel, name, express, and manage both the basic, innate affects (e.g., fear and anger) and the more differentiated and cognitively mediated affects (e.g., shame and love). Thus, just as the mother played this role in early childhood, the therapist facilitates the cycle of affective communication within the therapeutic relationship.

If we look at the child research for clues as to what our adult patients need, there is a plethora of information. Schore (1994) notes that as early as 60 years ago,

> the Russian psychologist Vygotsky (1978), studying the basic mechanism underlying the internalization of higher psychological functions, posited the general developmental principle that all psychological processes appear first at an interpersonal and only later at an intrapersonal level . . . all higher functions emerge as a result of social interaction [p. 358].

This is an amazing statement that, if true, validates not only the thera-peutic enterprise, but also the contemporary emphasis on the interper-sonal aspects of treatment. Vgotsky's theory supports the notion that intrapsychic change across a broad array occurs as a result of interpersonal exchanges, lending credence to the concept of a more active, expressive therapist. But is Vgotsky's theory supported by modern research? To a great degree, it is. Stern (1985), in reporting his research results, says:

> One conclusion is that the infant somehow makes a match between the feeling state as experience within and as seen "on" or "in" another, a match that we can call *interaffectivity.*
>
> Interaffectivity may be the first, most pervasive, and most imme-diately important form of sharing subjective experiences. Demos (1980, 1982a), Thoman and Acebo (1983), Tronick (1979), and others, as well as psychoanalysts, propose that early in life affects are both the primary *medium* and the primary *subject* of communi-cation [pp. 132–133].

The primary importance of affect continues as the infant evolves, and at around nine months, according to Stern, mothers naturally change the nature of their affective responses, moving from mere imitation of the infants' affect to responding with their own affective expressions. Stern says that "What is being matched is not the other person's behavior *per se,* but rather some aspect of the behavior that reflects the person's feeling state" (p. 142). He refers to this affective matching between mother and infant as "*affective attunement.*"

Although the literature on adults does not address the issue of affective attunement per se, the longstanding recognition of the therapeutic benefits of high-level empathy can be understood as a similar mechanism for promoting affective development in the therapeutic relationship. The analytic theory most compatible with a notion of the need for a life-long affective attunement with others would be Kohut's (1984) ideas regard-ing the never-ending need for mature selfobjects who, by definition, provide needed empathy and affective responding.

Stern (1985), Stolorow, Brandchaft, and Atwood (1987) and Stolo-row and Atwood (1992) emphasize that infants and children are heavily dependent on affective responses from their caretakers. Without affec-tive responses they lack internal organization and the ability to express and contain their own affective experiences. Stolorow and Atwood (1992) refer to Krystal (1988), stating that

> Krystal (1988) has suggested that a critical dimension of affective development is the evolution of affects from their early form, in which they are experienced as bodily sensations, into subjective states that can gradually be verbally articulated. . . .
>
> [A]ffects may fail to evolve from bodily states to feelings because, in the absence of validating responsiveness, they are never able to become symbolically articulated. Hence the person remains literally alexithymic [pp. 186, 187].

Alexithymia, of course, is the inability to express, differentiate, and name emotions (with the exception of occasional, angry outbursts) and usually results from childhood trauma. While most patients do not present with alexithymia, *most* patients are lacking in affect development in some significant way. Brown (1993) notes that developmental failures in affect may "manifest themselves in one or more areas: expression, experience, tolerance, verbalization, recognition, orientation, transformation, and consciousness of affective processes, respectively" (p. 43). So we are left with the knowledge that the "capacity for affective expression may be innate, but the capacity for affect experience unfolds in the course of development" (Brown, 1993, p. 6). As the child develops, he or she builds an increasing repertoire of emotions and learns that affects are a primary mode of communication, that they act as "signals for another person" (Krystal, 1988, p. 17). Children's abilities to accurately label and express their feelings are highly dependent on how often and to what degree their caretakers express their own feelings (Brody and Harrison, 1987). Krystal (1988) also tells us that a critical dimension of affective development is the "evolution of affects from their early form, in which they are experienced as bodily sensations, into subjective states that can gradually be verbally articulated" (p. 42). (He notes that alexithymic patients remain stuck at the level of experiencing affect only, or primarily, as physical sensations or symptoms.) The most significant aspect of affect that *does not change with development* is that "nothing becomes an emotion until it travels outside of the brain to the musculature and microcirculation of the face, there to be assessed and interpreted as an affective response" (Nathanson, 1996, p. 385). (Tomkins, 1962, of course, did the pioneering research on innate affect and its expression on the face.) So when we think we know what a patient is feeling by the look on his or her face, we are probably right. Just as the patient knows what we are feeling in the same way.

Much of the controversy regarding therapist self-disclosure has been based not just on the issue of "contamination" but also on the relative superficiality assumed in the verbal exchanges between therapist and patient. Where is the unconscious in all of this? Are we simply to assume that both analyst and patient actually know what each is feeling most of the time? The answer to that is no, of course not. An accurate reading of affect depends on both parties' trusting their visceral responses to, and sufficient ability to read, a variety of facial expressions. And these expressions will occur, even if one is unaware of them. My patient, Susan, who is alexithymic and almost always denies being angry, very often registers the facial expression documented by Tomkins (1962) as rage. And I find myself feeling uneasy and somewhat defended when she walks into her session wearing this facial expression, no matter what she says to me about what she is feeling. Her face and my gut reaction match each other and tell more truth than what she can always consciously know.

Another important aspect of the expression of emotion is that it is social (Parkinson, 1996) and, as such, often appears just as the patient enters the office. The expression has been saved for me, or occurs in response to me, for a specific purpose, whether or not the patient is aware of this purpose. Parkinson (1996) cites a study by Kraut and Johnston (1979), who observed bowlers and noted that they had one set of responses when they were facing the pins and quite a different set of responses when they turned to face the other bowlers, the latter responses being much more animated and expressive. When they were facing the pins, there was no point in registering any facial expressions, because there was no one to receive them. Parkinson cites this as evidence that emotions are social and serve as a form of communication. He says,

Many emotions have relational rather than personal meanings (e.g., deRivera, 1984) and the expression of these meanings in an emotional interaction serves specific interpersonal functions depending on the nature of the emotion . . . emotion is social through and through. Its fundamental basis in many cases is as a form of communication [p. 680].

Therefore, therapists and patients alike constantly register emotional reactions to each other, helping to inform each other of their true feelings, regardless of their conscious experience.

To summarize, infants and children learn to express their emotions freely, and ultimately, through their mothers' responses, learn how to name, differentiate, and manage them. Initially the mother typically only mirrors the child's rather basic expression, but as the child expands his or her repertoire the mother responds, not just with mirroring, but mixes in her own personal emotional response. As Thompson (1990) says, "Emotion is initially regulated by others, but over the course of early development it becomes increasingly self-regulated as a result of neuro-psychological development" (p. 371). Since these experiences are univer-sal, doesn't it seem likely that the therapist helping an adult with affective regulation problems would need to follow the same basic principles for facilitating affective regulation that are used in childhood? Both verbal and nonverbal interventions need to be appropriate for the adult patient, yet it is hard to imagine that the process for learning affect management would differ substantially regardless of the age of the patient. If we further consider that the route to intrapersonal development is relational, or interpersonal, then the affective attunement between analyst and patient becomes a critical variable in the therapeutic action.

Written on the Body

Although I concur with Stolorow, Atwood, and Krystal regarding the importance of reciprocal mutual influence for the regulation and integra-tion of affective experience, I *disagree* with the implied conclusion that children evolve into adults who rely primarily on symbolic articulation of affect—words. Certainly, if all goes well, the acquisition of language facilitates the regulation of affect, in that it gives the individual the opportunity to label, discuss, understand, and mediate affective states. A basic analytic tenet says that we use our intellect to help organize and regulate our affective experiences. Verbal expressions also allow some form of affective communication in instances when strong displays of emotion might be considered socially inappropriate and would therefore be punished.

[handwritten marginalia at top: "Re irony? in constructed paradigm — that awareness is a passive discernment phenom with expression"]

While acknowledging the inherent importance of developing the ability to label and discuss emotions rather than only experiencing them as bodily states, I disagree with the assumption that continued development negates the critical aspect of *physically experiencing emotions* to complete an affective communication. We all know that we experience feeling viscerally and that this is true throughout our lifetime. Our minds do not cue us that we are feeling something strongly; our bodies do. Our minds inquire as to the origin and meaning of that feeling, and help us to manage those feelings. But without the bodily sensation, there is no inquiry. (After all, even in adulthood the face remains the primary signaler of an affective event, rather than verbal expressions.)

Fast (1992) tried to recapture the importance of the body, as well as the mind, in her paper on mind-body and the relational perspective. She says that while Freud's notions of bodily involvement in emotional states were erroneous, he was correct in assuming a mind-body relationship. She notes that even though Freud understood well that infants cannot separate thought from bodily action, he chose to emphasize the later period when mental consideration preceded motoric action.

Fast credits Piaget for noting a mind-body period of development. But, like Freud, he proposed that normal development progresses to the point where the capacity for thought is free of the body. The implication is that emotion is registered intellectually, *in the mind,* rather than physically, *in the body,* if development occurs normally. Therefore, even though it is undoubtedly true that the capacity for verbalizing and cognitively mediating emotion evolves developmentally, the body never ceases to be a critical part of the emotion-signaling system, which Kelly (1996) describes as "critical for immediate, first-line survival" (p. 61).

Grotstein (1997) laments the separation of mind and body in analytic thinking, saying they are

> always inseparable but that they *seem* to lend themselves to the Cartesian artifice of disconnection so that we can conceive of one or another for the sake of discrimination. Put another way, I believe that the *mindbody* constitutes a single, holistic entity, one that we can think about and believe that we can imaginatively experience as being separate but that is mockingly *nonseparate* all the while [p. 205, all emphases by Grotstein].

Psychoanalysis, as it recognizes the importance of affect in human development, subsequently faces the task of re-integration of mind and body. What we know to be true is that patients who have been traumatized, and also the general population of personality disorders, demonstrate developmental failures in experiencing and managing affect. And these people represent a large percentage of those currently seeking treatment. Of course, it is no news to most clinicians that many of our patients suffer from the inability to experience and regulate their emotions. Much of the countertransference literature focuses on the affective onslaught one faces when treating many cases of narcissistic and borderline personality disorders. We have known for a long time that affect regulation is a problem that these patients bring to treatment and that presents a significant challenge to us as therapists. But I would have to add that I do not think we have been terribly successful in developing adequate theories and techniques for dealing with these patients. And the idea of using our bodily sensations as signals remains foreign.

To what extent do both our patients and ourselves use our bodies to register, and even communicate, deep emotions? I doubt that anyone could honestly say that he experiences a deep emotion without some observable accompanying physical sensation. And perhaps, in our desire to elevate the mind above the body, we have underestimated the role of the body in communication.

If we conceive of projective identification as primarily a body-to-body communication, then the simple containment of that affect by the analyst is insufficient on two grounds: one, letting the patient know that the communication has been received, and two, helping the patient to translate his emotional state into verbal representations—something that is essential to communication in the adult world. Understanding that the ability to verbalize affective states is a developmental achievement only partially acquired by many of our patients, we can naturally look more closely at body language, physical sensations, and projective identifications to help us understand and treat our patients. I think our resistance to "going first" when it comes to verbalized affective expressions often deprives our patients of the affective responding they need to further their own development.

We seem obsessed with the notion of "containment" of the patient's affect, which has limited value in terms of helping the patient with affect regulation. And I often wonder *who* or *what* we are really interested in containing. Discussions of therapist expression of affect at professional meetings often reflect a myriad of fears over what will happen if the analyst is overtly emotional. Terms like "out of control" and "potential for abuse" often drown out any serious discussion of how to use emotion constructively in the analytic setting.

Is Affect Inhibition Overvalued?

It seems that we have few problems diagnosing patients who suffer from the inability to contain and mediate their affective responses. These are the patients who often make our lives miserable as we attempt to cope with their emotional outbursts and impulsive behaviors. Unquestionably, treating people who are consistently out of control is challenging and stressful. But what about the patients who are *overcontrolled*? Do we worry less about them, and become complacent because they can provide an often much-needed respite from our patients who overwhelm us with their affective regulation problems?

In recent years Krystal (1988) and McDougall (1982) have raised our awareness of the patients who are alexithymic. Rather than presenting hysterically, these patients are very much in control and take pride in their cool, calm, collected manner, which society often rewards. Krystal says,

> What is deceptive to those unfamiliar with this disturbance is that these patients, who often function very successfully in their work, appear "superadjusted" to reality and lead one to expect excellent intellectual function. However, getting past the superficial impression of superb functioning, one uncovers a sterility and monotony of ideas and severe impoverishment of the imagination [p. 247].

Susan, the aforementioned patient whom I have chosen to use throughout this volume, certainly qualifies as alexithymic, arriving for her first session immaculately dressed, polite, pleasant, and appearing to function at a high level. When I asked her if she had ever been in treatment before, she related a history of four previous therapists, although none for any length of time, all of whom deemed her to be quite sane. One simply dismissed her as not needing therapy. And another took her as a lover, in part because she perceived Susan as wealthier, more successful, and more in control than she. The therapist's wish to be taken care of by Susan emerged soon after they began their affair. What made me aware that there was more to Susan than met the eye was her history and her current lack of emotional distress or insight regarding her life situation. You may recall that she came for therapy because she was unable to look for work and did not understand why. She was also socially isolated, lonely, and had no insight into her past failed relationships, including the affair with her last therapist. She showed no emotion when I questioned her about her past and expressed what I considered to be an unnatural lack of anger or regret over her therapist's abuse of her. She said that she dumped the therapist and had felt in control of the whole affair, so there was no reason to be upset. These attitudes told me that Susan had some very serious emotional problems, no matter how cool she seemed. In the sessions that followed over the next few months, Susan showed the same lack of emotion when she described her rather traumatic childhood, which included daily verbal and physical abuse by her parents. She described her mother as being completely emotionless, a "blank screen" who would not tolerate any show of emotion by her children, deeming it a "sign of weakness." Susan never remembered her dreams and literally did not know what I was talking about when I asked her about her fantasies.

Patients like Susan often spend years in psychoanalysis, dully repeating the details of their lives, but rarely getting any better. However, unless they regress (in which case all hell breaks loose), these patients do not demand our attention. Krystal (1988) notes that they come on time, pay their fees, and are generally responsible and undemanding. Yet their problems are just as serious as the patients who constantly demand that we notice them. Averill (1994) points out that

> The person who cannot express emotion in an open and effective manner when appropriate is as much out of control as is the person who habitually "lets it all hang out." Control implies the ability to respond in the way one wants, whether that entails the inhibition or expression of a response [p. 267].

I would add that it is not only what the person wants that is important, but also what is emotionally honest and what is optimally desirable at

the moment. But I agree with Averill that helping our inhibited, coop-
erative, and well-behaved patients to be more emotional should be as
important as helping our over-emotional patients to contain themselves.
The fact that society will reward the former but not the latter should not
cloud our clinical assessment of the patient's capacity for healthy affect
regulation.

Emotion and Cognition

First of all, all learning is facilitated through emotion. Contrary to what
many people believe, cognitive processing is effected significantly by
emotion. People are far more likely to remember something that elicited
an emotional reaction (Bower, 1994). Panskepp (1994) cites research
that demonstrates the critical role of emotion in all types of cognitive
functions:

> [T]he easiest way to light up higher mental processes—of thought,
> strategies, and conniving—is to activate basic emotional systems
> (Gray, 1990). When these basic systems have been aroused, then
> cognitive activity flows spontaneously [p. 313].

This information stands in stark contrast to the belief that emotions
hinder or prevent clear thinking, reasoning, and problem solving. Certainly excessive emotion impairs reality testing and good judgment, but
the optimal condition is ongoing, manageable emotional stimulation, not
the absence of strong feeling. Emotion plays an important role not only
in the quality of cognition, but also in the type. Clore (1994) says that

> findings suggest that emotion influences cognitive processing, per-
> haps in very fundamental ways. Positive affect appears to encourage
> unconstrained, heuristic processing, sometimes with creative re-
> sults, while sad affect seems to foster a focus on more controlled,
> systematic processing [p. 110].

So the nature of our feelings also determines the nature of our thoughts,
and vice versa. (The cognitive behaviorists have at least half of this
right.) The essential role of emotion in effective information processing

highlights not only the patient's need for ongoing, regulated affect, but also the therapist's. As I stated earlier in this volume, the analytic therapist who places too much emphasis on thoughts and interpretations, and avoids having strong feelings, cannot only fail to stimulate affective expression and management in her patients, but also will fail to *think optimally about the patient's condition and needs*. Just as mind and body cannot be separated, neither can feelings and thoughts.

Furthermore, the established relationship between emotion and cognition provides evidence that a good treatment needs to be an ongoing emotional event. If we accept that people change only when they can feel deeply and freely, when these feelings are responded to affectively by another person, and that both negative and positive affects provide opportunities for different types of cognitive processing, the responsibility for the analytic therapist to be emotionally involved, available, and expressive becomes greater.

What Is Emotional Memory?

Orange (1995) brought the concept of emotional memory to the forefront of analytic thinking. She says it "includes any form or part of experience that largely bypasses cognitive processes and carries significant residues from the intersubjective worlds of the past. Emotional memory has an unmediated quality that makes it feel compelling" (p. 113). She talks about how emotions can actually have a life of their own, which when I read it, seemed like a foreign idea to me. Didn't I just say that thoughts and feelings operate in concert? How then, can there be a strictly emotional memory? And what does emotional memory have to do with current functioning and the treatment situation?

For one thing, the concept of emotional memory is somewhat vague and unproven in the broad application that Orange provides. She built on the ideas of Emde, whom Clyman (1991) quotes regarding the idea of a recurrent pattern of affective experience. Clyman says that "Emde (1983) has suggested that there is a prerepresentational 'affective core of the self' which guarantees our sense of continuity across development in spite of the many ways we change" (p. 378). In other words, we have fairly stable ways of emotionally experiencing life that is not significantly altered by new experience. In this sense, a core affective pattern would be part of a necessary homeostasis, a notion supported by Schore (1994).

> Early object relational experiences thus directly influence the emergence of a frontolimbic system in the right hemisphere that can adaptively autoregulate both positive and negative affect in response to changes in the socioemotional environment. . . . The core of the self lies in patterns of affect regulation that integrates a sense of self across state transitions, thereby allowing for a continuity of inner experience [p. 33].

So there is clinical and experimental evidence that stable affective patterns, as well as specific affective reactions, exist and are called forth by stimuli that somehow mimic the original event. And Freud, once again, turns out to have known quite a bit. He hypothesized that we tended to recreate the same emotional scenarios over and over again, although he did not know at the time that affect-laden experiences actually have their own independent storehouse in the brain, ready to be recalled at an instant. I would add to this that the re-experiencing of past, intense affect is always a visceral event that is part of what makes it so real in the present, even if it entails some cognitive distortion so that it can be ordered up. For example, in the case of Susan, when she lies down on the couch and talks to me about how abusive her parents were, she begins to have these feelings all over again. The fact that her parents would throw her down on the floor and stand over her, sometimes slapping her, only increases the intensity of her equating the analytic process (lying on the couch, with me slightly away and above her in my chair) with her most negative early childhood experiences. Susan honestly feels at those moments that I am abusing her just as her parents did. She is swept away by her emotional memories and the visceral reenactment she experiences. In her mind, I must hold and comfort her to prove that I am different from her parents and not taking sadistic delight in her agony.

LeDoux (1994) tells us that it is important to distinguish between emotional memory and memory of emotion:

> The latter is a declarative, conscious memory of an emotional experience. It is stored as a fact about an emotional episode.

Emotional memory (mediated by the amygdala) and memory of emotion (mediated by the hippocampus) can be reactivated in parallel on later occasions. . . . In summary, emotional and declarative memory about emotion are mediated by different brain systems. These systems operate simultaneously and parallel during experiences. As a result, we can have conscious insight into our emotions and emotional memories . . . without emotions, one would have to learn the positive and negative stimulus value of situations through strictly cognitive means [p. 312].

So our emotional memory reminds us of the importance, or lack of importance, danger or safety, of everything in our environment. Emotional memory allows for homeostasis, but it is also a keystone of the phenomenon of "learning from one's experience." As LeDoux says, our emotional memory tells us immediately what to do, saving us the trouble of thinking through every new situation. On the less adaptive side, it may also instruct us to avoid some person, place or thing that reminds us of something unpleasant from the past that may, in reality, offer something positive that our emotional memory blinds us to.

Once again, Freud has been vindicated, in the sense that he posited transference as an established pattern of relating and emotional responding that is cued by something in the present, but oftentimes calls up both an affective state and thoughts that may have more to do with past experience than present ones. And even though Freud intuitively understood the importance of reliving these affective states, he incorrectly concluded that the patient could *cathart* and achieve new insights and patterns of relating. Not being privy to the mechanisms for early affective expression and regulation, he could not know that the analyst's emotional participation was critical to the patient's success in recognizing, expressing, and integrating affective states. He had half the equation, perhaps because the whole equation places such great personal demands on the analyst. (If eye contact was too stressful for Freud, how could he conceive of a day marked by one emotional exchange after another?) The type of emotional availability I am discussing requires so much energy and attention from the analyst, as well as self-awareness, that it severely limits the number of patients that anyone could see in a given day. Thus, practicing this way is not only potentially personally threatening, but also places significant limits on the analyst's personal income.

Affect, Alexithymia, and Trauma

The uses of emotion are particularly important when treating patients who have suffered early trauma. Krystal (1988, 1997) has alerted us to the needs of the patients he describes as alexithymic—those who cannot recognize, or label or express emotions other than occasional outburts of rage. He says these patients typically have been traumatized in childhood, causing them to develop into adulthood without the essential tools for expressing and containing emotions. Although the burgeoning literature on incest and other "survivors" seems to place great value on recalling past abuses, it seems that the more essential hurdle facing an individual who suffered early trauma is the identification, expression, and management of affect in the present.

If we integrate what we know about individuals who have been traumatized with Krystal's portrait of the alexithymic patient, we are left with the person who is hypervigilant, overattending to the slightest detail of the analyst's behavior or deportment, yet unaware of his or her own moods and feelings. These patients cannot answer when asked how they are feeling. As a result, they often defensively change the topic to some observation of the analyst, or they respond with what they know, usually a physical feeling or symptom. The patient may say he or she feels a weight on the chest, a stomach tied up in knots, or a current worry about having cancer, AIDS, or some other potentially fatal condition. Stuck at the level of physical processing of emotion, rather than integrating physical sensation with cognitive awareness and a language for feelings, the alexithymic patient stays away from the topic of his or her own emotions. Earlier I quoted Krystal's observation that alexithymic patients often present as "super-adjusted," preferring to remain cool and calm at all times, and often believing that any show of emotion is a sign of weakness that will be seized as an opportunity to destroy the patient.

Thus Krystal's alexithymic patient and McDougall's psychosomatic patient, as well as the myriad numbers of patients identified as having experienced early trauma, seem to have a great deal in common and be drawn from the same general pool. They somatize rather than cathart, are hypervigilant, and are lacking in basic trust. They often use projective identification as a way of communicating with their therapists, essentially letting the therapist know, "This is what I am feeling." They trust their intuition and their bodies more than their feelings, which are often just a blur of "feeling upset," and often need their analysts to self-disclose or make physical contact with them as a way of facilitating both trust and emotional communication. (See the final section of this chapter for more discussion of the clinical implications.)

Gender Differences

Finally, how are men and women different in their experience and expression of affect? Social stereotypes proclaim women as the emotional gender and men as the stoics, yet the literature on alexithymic patients refers primarily to women. If women who have been traumatized at an early age have little access to their emotions, then we have a rather large group of women who clearly defy the sexual stereotype. Yet Brody (1993) says that there is increasing evidence to support the idea that women express their emotions more intensely, both verbally and nonverbally (facial expressions), than men do. Another interesting finding reported by Brody is that "males are more intensely emotionally expressive through actions and behaviors than are females" (pp. 113–114). In other words, if a man feels strongly about something, he wants to act on that feeling in some way, while women are more content restricting themselves to verbal expressions of emotion. As I read this I couldn't help but wonder if this helps to explain why the analytic literature (overwhelmingly dominated by male authors) historically reflects fears of analysts being out of control and acting out if they attempt to self-disclose their countertransference feelings. Could it be that these fears of acting out reflect a gender difference in emotional expression, since women typically violate the boundaries less often than men do, and do not seem to be as concerned about self-disclosure as a slippery slope?

Of course, this does not mean that we should simply dismiss the male analyst's concern about acting out. It might be fair to say that women are more likely to be comfortable with expressing their emotional responses to patients, and less likely to commit boundary violations—yet this would certainly be less likely among female therapists who had their own history of trauma and/or alexithymia. It could be equally as fair to say that male analysts (knowing their own predilection for acting on their feelings) need to be more cautious and monitor their own inclinations more carefully to preserve the boundaries. Yet the many male therapists who

know they are comfortable with verbal expressions of their feelings
certainly would not need to concern themselves as much with the gender
difference findings.

Clinical Implications

Whether or not the gender differences in expressing emotion account
for the reluctance of analysts to be more emotionally expressive, there is
no doubt that therapists' expression of emotion has been a very controversial topic in recent years. Even the intersubjective theorists such as
Stolorow and Atwood (1992) remain convinced of the need for abstinence on the analyst's part, in spite of their recognition of the role of
"reciprocal mutual influence" (p. 18) in any intersubjective field. While
these authors criticize Mitchell and others for failing to acknowledge the
influence of the analyst on the process, their case material reads much
like any other, with their theoretical stand being used to enlighten the
analyst's interpretations rather than create a field of mutual, yet asymmetrical, affective communication. Stolorow and Atwood seem to believe that empathy alone will provide the interventions needed for the
emergence of repressed affective states. But my question remains, how
do you relate empathically to an *unexpressed* emotion?
   Basch (1991), with reference to a narcissistic patient he was treating,
makes the point that more active interventions are needed to help the
patient recognize and express split-off affect, although he is not explicit
in his recommendations.

> The analyst's affective abstinence that serves us so well with the
> psychoneurotic patient would only have played into the defense of
> a patient like Mr. W., a patient with a narcissistic character disor-
> der. Since disavowal interferes with affective recognition and matu-
> ration in the area of the patient's pathology, it is pointless to play
> the waiting game and trust that, sooner or later, the patient will
> transfer what needs to be analyzed [p. 301].

In a similar vein, Krystal (1988) points to the limitations of conventional
technique:

[C]onsideration of the energizing aspects of emotions provides both
a rationale for and a recognition of the need to reintegrate and
self-regulatory activities as part of the psychotherapeutic work. At
the same time it alerts us to the fact that classical (perhaps more
accurately, "conventional") psychoanalytic technique may be missing a vital aspect of the patient's and therapist's function. Rather
than taking an idealistic view of the purity of technique, we might
better direct that idealism to pursuing the goal of the patient's
greater self-integration [p. 125].

Thus both Basch and Krystal have noted that many of the people we
treat will simply not make very much progress in the area of affective
recognition and expression without direct affective interventions by the
therapist. Although I discuss the specifics of self-disclosure in the following chapter, there is no question that affective interventions certainly
require therapists' disclosure of felt emotion. I previously (Maroda, 1991,
1995b) outlined guidelines for therapist disclosure that allow for both
emotional responses elicited by the patient's question of "How are you
feeling toward me right now?" and for revelation of affect experienced as
the result of projective identification. The above authors' discussion of
the patient's split-off affect lends itself to further discussion of how the
therapist facilitates the patient's experience of his or her own disavowed
feelings. McDougall (1978), in discussing the way some patients attempt
to influence their analysts, says that

> Rather than seeking to communicate moods, ideas, and free asso-
> ciations, the patient seems to aim at making the analyst *feel* some-
> thing or stimulating him to *do* something: this "something" is
> incapable of being named and the patient himself is totally unaware
> of this aim [p. 179].

From my own experience, I would say that McDougall's "something" is
usually the experience and expression of the patient's split-off affect.
Unable to bear their own feelings, many patients seek to have their
analysts feel and express these feelings for them, so they can find them
acceptable and learn to do this for themselves. For the therapist to deny
the patient this essential experience, which we can liken to the mother's
early affective responding to the infant, is to deprive the patient of an

essential step in his or her affective development. Interpretations given when affect is needed amounts to anti-communication, resulting in the patient getting worse.

That is why so many patients accuse their therapists of being unresponsive no matter how concerned those therapists might genuinely be, or how hard they try. Often anything short of an affective response does not count, or register, at all for the patient. He will behave as if no response was given by the therapist, or will accuse the therapist of deliberately withholding the sought-after response. Things become understandably complicated, as McDougall says, when the patient, asked what he wants, often says he does not know, due to his having repressed the affect he is seeking to find through his analyst.

Just as our early emotional development depended on receiving affective responses from others, so does our continued development. Most certainly for those who are seeking what amounts to a remedial emotional education when they come for treatment, the affective responses of the therapist are critical for completing the cycle of affective communication.

When I read case histories I am often dismayed to discover how often therapists describe getting control of themselves after being strongly stimulated by a patient, carefully making sure that they do not express emotion when responding. If the patient is stimulating anger, for example, the therapist will wait for the wave of anger to pass, and then as cooly and calmly as possible say, "I think you would like me to feel as angry as you do." Implicit in such a response is, "But don't think for a minute that I'm going to. You can spend your entire session trying to provoke me, but I will never give you the satisfaction of seeing me angry."

When I read things like this, I always think to myself, "Why not?" Why not show the patient exactly how angry you are? What is the point of withholding emotion and thwarting the patient in his quest for affective communication? As I have stated previously (1995b) he will only have to up the ante next time, until he finally gets an emotional response or gives up in despair and subsequent depressed withdrawal.

Traditionally, analytic clinicians have believed that any personal responses would only detract form the patient's experience. This made some sense if you believed that analysis was primarily an intrapsychic event. But it makes much less sense if you believe that analytic treatment is not only both intrapsychic and interpersonal, but that (as stated earlier in this chapter) the order of developmental progression dictates that the interpersonal necessarily occurs first, with the intrapsychic following.

If the patient repeatedly stimulates a strong emotion or visceral response in the analyst, then it is probably time for an affective response. So long as the therapist is reasonably in control and behaves responsibly, the show of emotion should not be damaging to the patient. (In the next chapter I address questions regarding the analyst's pathology at work, potentially coloring his affective experience of the patient.)

In reviewing the literature on affect I found an interesting chapter on affect and intimacy (Kelly, 1996) that focused chiefly on couples' intimate relationships. In this context Kelly discusses the negative outcome that results when individuals do not respond honestly with feeling to each other. Yet when I read it I was struck by how much it equally applied to the therapeutic dyad.

> All close relationships require proximity that causes us to step on each other's toes. If, for whatever reason, one does not say "ouch" and communicate the distress experienced as a result of the other's actions, a complex dilemma is created. The need to disguise the distress causes the inmost self to be hidden from the other. The distress, if unrelieved, eventually triggers anger and resentment that must also be hidden. This causes further withdrawal and hiding of the inmost self. The other, perhaps not even aware of the offense, experiences feeling of rejection triggered by the withdrawal, without information adequate to allow reestablishment of the intimate bond. Now hurt, this other may also resort to withdrawal, thus setting in motion a recursive loop of rejection and hurt [pp. 87–88].

Looking at the research on affect necessitates the question: In thwarting our patients in their quest for an emotional response from us, have we unknowingly been withholding that which could be most therapeutic? We might be tempted to rationalize our lack of overt emotional expression, on the old grounds that we will detract from the patient's experience, but this fails to address the change process. I have claimed that the patient often will be unable to ever name his own affective experience if the therapist does not feel and name it first. Likewise, Schore (1994) says that

The psychotherapist's establishment of a dyadic affective "growth promoting environment" influences the ontogeny of homeostatic self-regulatory systems (Greenspan, 1981). Towards this end, both positive and negative classes of affect need to be transacted and regulated in the therapist-patient relationship [p. 463].

In other words, affect research suggests that emotional exchanges between therapist and patient are critical to the patient's growth and development. He states further that

Affect regulatory dialogs mediated by a psychotherapist may induce literal structural change in the form of new patterns of growth of cortical-limbic circuitries, especially in the right hemisphere which contains representation of self-and-object images [p. 469].

It stands to reason that if emotional exchanges, or lack of, created the affective patterns that a person creates over and over again, that only new emotional exchanges could facilitate the altering of old affective patterns. Changes in thoughts affect cognitive patterns in the brain, and new emotional exchanges create new emotional memories and affective patterns in the brain.

If we remember that emotion is the most basic form of communication, and is essentially relational, then perhaps we can rid ourselves of the notion that the therapist's expression of felt emotion is somehow inappropriate or damaging. Krystal (1988) has suggested that therapists' difficulty in treating alexithymic patients may be due to the frequency with which they suffer from the problem themselves. Obviously only returning to treatment could address the problems of the alexithymic therapist.

From my experience there are more therapists who have painfully sat on their emotions, erroneously believing that they were doing the right thing. For these therapists, the prospect of using their emotional responses constructively for the patient's development is a potentially rewarding and mutually healthy experience. Understanding that the withholding of felt emotion can be just as harmful as any affective expression, given its covert nature, perhaps we can explore the therapeutic nature of affect, freeing both our patients and ourselves.

Chapter 4

Why
Self-Disclosure Works in Spite of the
Analyst's Limitations

How much does the patient really need to know about the analyst? And what type of information is most helpful? Many people resist the notion of self-disclosure, convinced that the analyst will inevitably create a persona that serves to defend against the patient's experience as much as anything else. Others fear that the patient will be burdened by what may amount to the analyst's thinly-veiled attempts to get her own needs met. We used to believe that patients inevitably attempted to lead us astray; now we seem to think that analysts inevitably will do the same to their patients. And I cannot help but wonder why we seem so intent on ascribing negative motivations and destructiveness to one or another members of the therapeutic relationship. Perhaps because we are all too familiar with the negative feelings we often harbor toward our patients, and thus worry that we will do them harm if we become more expressive. The point of this chapter is that harboring negative feelings does, in fact, do more harm than acknowledging them, and that our personal weakness and faults need not prevent us from generally doing right by the patient.

This chapter explores the use of self-disclosure, including a review of current opinions regarding its use, why I think it is an essential tool for any clinician, and also how it can be misused.

Over the years the concept of therapeutic self-disclosure has appeared, and disappeared, in the analytic literature. Some early contributors like Ferenczi (1932), Little (1951, 1957), and Tauber (1954) argued strongly for disclosure, while Heimann (1950) and Reich (1950) argued just as strongly against it. Langs (1978), Greenson (1967), Gill (1982), Kohut (1971, 1977), and Stolorow, Brandchaft and Atwood (1987) favor acknowledging mistakes when pressed by the patient to admit them, but do not favor other self-disclosures. Searles (1979) made the case for disclosure eloquently, but restricted his technique to hospitalized borderline and schizophrenic patients.

More recently, Tansey and Burke (1989), Bollas (1987), Aron (1991, 1992, 1996), and Renik (1995) favor occasional disclosure. The "occasional disclosure" stance is a moderate one that helps bypass the "wild analysis" insult so often thrown at clinicians who attempt to bring the analyst into the process in a more personal way. Of late, however, the increasing acceptance of the two-person paradigm not only legitimizes self-disclosure, but recognizes its inherent place in this paradigm and demands a new perspective on technique that uses disclosure responsibly.

Moving from the point of view that sees personal disclosures as burdensome to the patient, intrusive, and indicative of an incomplete personal analysis, to the point of view that sees disclosure as respected technique that is invaluable to a successful treatment, is not an easy transition to be sure. Analytic clinicians rightly question the proper use of self-disclosure and fear the unseemly gratifications that fuel their worst nightmares, not to mention possible malpractice actions. One patient asks if you love him, another if you are married with children, another if you wish the hour was over, another if you are sexually aroused at this particular moment in time. On this latter point, the patient notes that as you remain silent you are blushing. Some days it is enough to make you run screaming for analytic abstinence.

No doubt things were easier when all you had to do, when what you were analytically *compelled* to do, was compassionately refuse the patient's pleas for feedback, reassurance, personal data, and last but not least, a sign that he had an impact on you—that he could make you feel something. In those days you forced yourself to be still, to say nothing, to remain motionless in your chair when you felt like squirming, to clench your jaw when you felt like screaming. You did it because you thought it was the right thing, even though you suffered when the hour was finally over and the patient left the room. You suffered the martyr's fate when you didn't tell a patient that you loved him, you escaped your guilt when you didn't tell a patient that you hated him, and you escaped unbearable vulnerability when you didn't tell a patient that you needed him. But you also didn't sleep those nights, lost some patients who continued to haunt you, and heard a small voice challenging the "rightness" of what you were doing. You consoled yourself with the ascetic's reassurance—that anything worth doing is worth suffering for.

And now you are being released from this prison of traditional psychoanalysis. You are being told that revealing a little feeling now and then is a good thing. But the problem persists of how to bring the analyst more fully into the analytic encounter without sacrificing the sacred privilege of the patient to have a "room of one's own," a place that suspends social convention enough to promote a degree of self-exploration unequaled in any other relationship.

Most of us welcome the idea of becoming more human, and more present, in the analytic relationship—but recoil at the notion of transforming analysis into *just another relationship*. In fact, both Renik (1995) and Greenberg (1995) have recently observed that one of the reasons we so tenaciously hold on to the notion of some type of anonymity is because historically this has been what distinguishes us from other "healers." We take pride in our high-minded desire not to mesmerize or otherwise influence our patients in a guru-like manner. Psychoanalysis has consistently identified a certain lack of personal presence or persuasion as being at the heart of our integrity and commitment to facilitating the growth and prosperity of our patients rather than ourselves. Now that we are faced with the two-person paradigm, we search for ways to maintain the integrity, and sanctity, of the analytic setting while maximizing our personal usefulness to the patient.

While reviewing the literature on self-disclosure, it became clear to me both how rapidly we are changing our views on self-disclosure, and also how much we are remaining the same. As little as ten years ago the notion of deliberate self-disclosure, other than the need to explain lengthy absences by the analyst or to prepare for the analyst's pregnancy, illness, or death, was nothing short of heresy. Slowly, this attitude has changed as the two-person paradigm has gained in acceptance. Both Renik and Aron, noted earlier for their acceptance of "occasional disclosure" have made the transition to advocating disclosure as a consistent component of technique (Renik, 1995; Aron, 1995)—something that both Ehrenberg and myself have advocated for a number of years (1991). At the same time Greenberg (1995), among others, has maintained his ambivalent feelings about self-disclosure,

> even in moments when we are telling our patients about ourselves we are, consciously or unconsciously, deciding what not to say. It may be that self-revelation is inevitable, but—certainly when we move beyond disclosing bare facts to talking about our beliefs or feelings—there is also something mythic about it. And because it is mythic, the idea of self-revelation itself can be misleading and even dangerous clinically. Both patient and analyst believe that when the analyst shares a personal thought or a feeling something has been given and they collusively ignore what has been withheld [p. 196].

Somehow the notion that the analyst's self-revelations are *mythic* while the patient's are ordinary, seems oddly grandiose and incorrect to me. Patients may be startled at hearing a self-disclosure from an analyst who is not normally forthcoming, thus infusing it with a measure of uniqueness and power that does not properly belong to it. But this added weight to the analyst's self-disclosure is easily lifted through its more regular and normal use.

Greenberg also cautions against self-disclosure because, "I am not necessarily in a privileged position to know, much less to reveal, everything that I think or feel" (p. 197). Both of his statements about self-disclosure are grounded in a philosophical approach that one associates more with an authoritarian posture. A more egalitarian position that advocates mutuality frees both analyst and patient, in that the analyst no longer needs to be perfect, all-knowing, or mythic. At the same time, the patient is freed from being ignorant, pathological, and hopelessly unaware.

Levenson (1996) has recently argued that the analyst cannot reliably reveal his countertransference because the troublesome emotional responses to the patient are almost always out of the analyst's awareness and typically reveal themselves through some acting out on the analyst's part. I disagree with the first half of this statement, and agree with the second. As I stated earlier, most analysts *are* aware of their disturbing countertransference feelings but suppress or repress them out of shame, embarrassment, fears of being out of control, or fear of being vulnerable to the patient. As a result of sweeping this material under the rug, analysts often discover their own countertransference as it unexpectedly surfaces in some untoward emotional outburst. Wouldn't it be better to reveal this material as a matter of course rather than waiting for it to build beyond the analyst's tolerance and burst forth like some alien within? Doing so would certainly enhance the analyst's feelings of being responsibly in control of himself while conducting the treatment.

Josephs (1995) also opposes disclosure of the countertransference for reasons similar to Greenberg's and Levenson's. Referring to faith in the usefulness of therapist self-disclosure as "naive realism," he says,

> Since any affect can serve to defend against any other affect, advocates of using countertransference as important information about the analytic relationship caution against using countertransference oracularly. Oracular use of countertransference implies that the analyst's feelings never serve a defensive function but are always an accurate reading of the patient's psyche [p. 348].

He goes on to say that we are in danger of taking our personal, and perhaps idiosyncratic, affective responses as truths rather than biased responses. Again, I agree and disagree. There is no disputing that our subjectivity effects everything we do and think, and that we must continually examine our experience in this light. Yet wholesale elimination of self-disclosure because it is inevitably personal and selective in its nature both fails to address the powerful therapeutic potential of expressed affect and "naively" presumes that interpretation and other analytic interventions *do not* suffer from an equal degree of bias or distortion.

Spezzano (1993) notes that, regardless of what we do with the affective communications we receive, they have great value in spite of the inherent limitations surrounding unconscious processes.

> The unconscious processes that produce affective states are never fully available even to the conscious scrutiny of the patient in whom they have occurred; they are even less immediately available to the analytic observer and listener. The analyst will inevitably receive the affective product of these processes with her own unconscious and will then be limited to conscious scrutiny of what emerges into her own preconscious-conscious flow of psychic events. Out of the imperfect scrutiny, however, will emerge usable information about, first, the affective state of the patient and, second, those unconscious processes out of which it originated [p. 211].

We could also apply Spezzano's observations to the analyst's affective communication and the patient's response to it.

If we approach self-disclosure by the analyst from the old, authoritarian perspective that desires perfection, surely we will get nowhere. Anyone who regularly uses self-disclosure will tell you that the analyst inevitably shows more humanity, weakness, and vulnerability, rather than strength, surety, and authority. And perhaps it is this very vulnerability that provides the most resistance to the notion of self-disclosure.

Old ways of thinking about ourselves die hard. Only a few years ago we were supposed to strive for perfection. On the surface, this may seem like an easy, even relieving, attribute to sacrifice. But is it? While we may welcome the opportunity to admit to loving our patients or wishing we could do more for them, and wanting the best for them—we may not be so desirous of admitting that we also hate them, are competitive with them, feel demoralized when we are constantly criticized and de-idealized, and may feel abandoned when they announce they are ready to leave us. Although these feelings are easy to identify as only human, they certainly have not been noted as such when felt by analysts toward their patients.

Few clinicians write about having negative feelings toward their patients, and when they do, it is usually accompanied by a confession of guilt and shame. The old analytic prototype never worked, *could never work*, because it relied on us being more than human, an impossible transcendence. The fact that for decades we deluded ourselves and our patients into thinking that a successful analysis could render a person as "perfectly analyzed" and therefore, "perfectly human" has not stopped us from wanting and hoping that we could somehow make this true.

And nowhere in our training were we ever prepared for feeling unrelenting lust, sadism, rage, envy or a desire to keep our patients from having more than we have. Feeling any of these things was said to mean that we were "insufficiently analyzed," and therefore unable to maintain the fantasied level of evenly hovering attention—undisturbed by passion or pettiness.

Small wonder that the idea of revealing our feelings, particularly our negative ones, sends us reeling back to the security of anonymity. The one-person paradigm may be quickly slipping into history, but our guilt, shame, embarrassment, and *relative unfamiliarity* with experiencing our own primitive feelings, is not. The reality of the two-person paradigm appears to be much easier to accept on a theoretical level than it is at a clinical one. Analysts still clinging to the notion that they should be healthier and more virtuous than they are, embrace the relational model as an intellectual process informing the analyst's interpretations. I think this is a misuse of the interpersonal realities that denies the mandate to bring the analyst into the process in a more personal and active way.

Defining Technique

There is a marked tendency in the analytic literature to give case examples and note what worked well, or perhaps failed, in a particular therapy situation. But prescriptions or guidelines for technique are rarely given, perhaps to avoid criticism or the appearance of arrogance or authoritarianism. Yet we all know that some interventions *do* work better than others, even if only with a particular type of patient in a specific situation. In general, we are more comfortable talking about what *not to do*, such as socialize with patients, fail to collect the fees, or behave in a way that is not *analytic*. On this latter point, it is difficult to escape judgment unless one fails ever to say exactly what one said or did, which has become the norm. As a result, we have no real framework for the use of self-disclosure. However, many of the current voices on this topic actually *discourage* the formulation of theoretical and clinical guidelines, fearing that they will become reified as "rules."

The list of those reluctant or opposed to setting down guidelines for self-disclosure includes Jacobs (1995), who says that "self-disclosure cannot be prescribed as a general technique" (p. 245); Greenberg (1995), who says "it is not particularly useful to attempt to come up with any sweeping statement about self-disclosure. I do not see any advantage to covering a wide range of situations with a one-size-fits-all technical prescription" (p. 197); and Aron (1996), who advocates the use of self-disclosure but nonetheless says, "I am concerned that what are meant as guidelines may be taken as rules, and that this mistaken use may prevent further useful clinical exploration" (p. 243).

Although I am sympathetic to the concern that any new innovations may, and probably will, become as reified as the way we practiced in the past, I do not agree that this is a good enough reason to avoid creating a useful context for the use of self-disclosure, or any other technique. How many therapists are confident enough to learn merely from their own experimentation? Most people are rightfully hesitant to try anything new without adequate understanding of how to use it. And how are we to train new therapists if all we provide is permission to self-disclose with no suggestions regarding how and when to do it?

For me, it makes more sense to look closely at what people have found to work and tease out the underlying principles that apply to forming reasonable guidelines. If we emphasize that these are, after all, guidelines rather than imperatives, we can encourage new therapists to use their own best judgment to modify the techniques with individual patients, who will surely defy the expectations at one turn or another.

As Renik (1995) says, "I will suggest that we can benefit from a more systematic consideration of useful forms of self-disclosure by the analyst that currently have to be bootlegged in and around the edges of a theory of technique which in principle discourages them" (p. 467). In the interests of replacing the "bootlegging" Renik refers to, I want to examine the guidelines I provided nine years ago in *The Power of Countertransference*, acknowledging that I begged off on certain issues because of the controversy surrounding self-disclosure at that time. I also want to acknowledge some of the criticism of those guidelines that I think is reasonable. Most importantly, I want to re-establish the notion that guidelines are not only helpful, they are essential to promoting the learning and implementation of new techniques.

In the case of self-disclosure I have attempted to place its use within the framework of completing the cycle of affective communication with the patient, which I consider to be the most important application. This is not to diminish some of the other reasons to disclose, noted by Gorkin (1987), and cited by me in 1991. These include confirming the patient's sense of reality; establishing the therapist's genuineness, honesty, or humanness; clarifying the impact the patient is having on the therapist and others; and ending treatment impasses. And these reasons are certainly compatible with the overarching theme of affective communication.

In my previous work I emphasized that self-disclosure works best if it focuses primarily on feeling rather than extraneous personal information, which I still believe to be true. I believe that the emotional reality between therapist and patient is the essential dynamic that needs to be explored. Aron (1996) and others have objected to this guideline based on having success with giving personal information to patients that seemed necessary to contextualize or explain the feelings the analyst was having at the time, and I do not disagree with his comments. In fact, I think it is often the case that the patient will ask where a particular attitude or fear originated in the analyst's own history. And over the years that I have been disclosing my feelings to patients I have often confided this type of personal information (such as being a twin, or having been dominated by a very strong-willed older sister, etc.) to help them understand why I feel the way I do in certain situations. Naturally, I feel more compelled to provide this information the more my emotional responses to the patient are colored by my own history. In this way I can be honest about my feelings toward the patient while still taking responsibility for what originated in me. But nine years ago I was reluctant to give this advice, fearing that therapists inexperienced in the technique would take the easier road of giving information about themselves rather than responding emotionally to their patients. In *The Power of Countertransference*, I said: "The therapist must disclose whatever is necessary to facilitate the patient's awareness and acceptance of the truth" (Maroda, 1991, p. 87). I stand by that advice while admitting that this may very well require the disclosure of personal information, but usually as an adjunct to an emotional response.

Ferenczi's (1932) early experiments with mutual analysis demonstrated that there is such a thing as too much disclosure on the analyst's part, and that any degree of mutual analysis is unworkable. He clearly observed that it was the disclosure of his negative feelings toward his patient "RN" that was therapeutic rather than giving her the opportunity to analyze him.

Regarding the use of disclosure by the analyst on an intuitive basis, rather than in direct response to the patient's requests or provocations, I do think this area of technique belongs more correctly to the experienced therapists who have already practiced extensively with self-disclosure at the patient's behest. The therapist's intuitive use of self-disclosure is the one area that cannot really be taught, and relies heavily on sound judgment, a strong connection to the patient, a high degree of self-awareness, and an experienced-based self-trust in identifying that critical moment when a disclosure is needed. The only practical advice that I give to experienced therapists is to consider using self-disclosure when they find themselves distancing from the patient for any length of time, either during the course of a single session or over a number of sessions. (This should occur, however, only after a period of self-inquiry about why the analyst has withdrawn. If the attempted self-analysis fails to allow the analyst to make herself emotionally available, then I would consider self-disclosure to break what amounts to an empathic impasse.) I make the point that no therapy can take place if there is no empathic connection, if the analyst has emotionally withdrawn. Although we may withdraw many times during the course of a session for a variety of good and bad reasons, ideally these moments are short-lived. In the interests of restoring communication, I advise therapists to examine what they are feeling during periods where they have felt the need to remove themselves from the interaction and ask themselves what they might say that would be emotionally honest and could potentially restore the connection with the patient.

Aron (1996) has disagreed with my statement that few patients require disclosure of the countertransference in any in-depth way during the early phases of treatment. Again, this was meant as a general statement, not an absolute. There are, indeed, some patients who ask many questions from the very beginning, often because they have been traumatized in the past and are testing the therapist for honesty and genuineness. But I would add the caveat that sometimes patients who ask many questions early in the treatment know they are stimulating negative feelings in the analyst and ask for this to be verified, or are finding fault in the analyst with some regularity and pressing for admissions of weakness. In either event the result is a re-creation of an earlier sadomasochistic pattern of relating. Thompson (1964) said on this topic,

> it is very important not to begin the truthtelling on the part of the analyst too early. One must not offer oneself as a sacrifice to the patient's sadism. Also it is necessary, first, that the patient feel sufficiently secure and have some confidence in his own powers before he is called on to face the defects in the one on whom he leans [p. 71].

Lastly, I have been quoted frequently as being against disclosure of the erotic countertransference, mostly by Gabbard. But this does not accurately represent my view. What I said was that I agreed with those who found that disclosure of the erotic countertransference was easily overstimulating and threatening, and therefore was not therapeutic in *most* instances. But I specifically cited a case where I thought that the therapist in question *should* have revealed his sexual feelings toward the patient.

Many people are still reluctant to use self-disclosure, mostly out of legitimate concerns or fears about using it productively for the patient. It seems that most of our fears fall into the categories of (1) not knowing when to disclose, (2) not knowing how to disclose, (3) conversely, not knowing when to keep quiet, and (4) risking that we may misrepresent ourselves to our patients and harm them through our defensiveness or lack of self-awareness.

Let me begin by referring the reader to my earlier work, where I outline how and when to disclose the countertransference in detail (Maroda, 1991), advocating using the patient as a consultant in his or her own case. Doing so virtually eliminates the concerns that many people have regarding whether or not the patient will be burdened or intruded on by a particular disclosure. Following the patient's lead allows for disclosure occurring as part of a mutual encounter rather than disclosure as an intervention the therapist must decide upon strictly on his own. I agree

with the criticism that disclosure done purely on the basis of the therapist's intuition will no doubt often occur at a time, or in a manner, that
is not in the patient's best interests.

However, the issues of how and when to disclose are not as difficult as
they might seem. Our patients do find ways to tell us what they need, and
they do this through two major avenues. One, they simply tell us directly.
Patients who have a therapeutic need to hear how the analyst is feeling
will persist in questioning the therapist in a heartfelt and sincere way. If
the analyst is unsure as to whether he or she should answer a particular
question, I advise simply asking the patient, "Do you really want me to
answer that question?" Questions that are defensive, intrusive or rhetori-
cal, of course, are not simply answered. As Epstein (1995) said in
discussing a patient whose questions he apparently answered too easily,

> Eventually when she would spontaneously ask me a direct ques-
> tion, she learned to protect herself from the danger that I might
> give her a direct answer by immediately admonishing me, "Don't
> answer that!" And eventually she cured me of such lapses to the
> point that she could depend on my remembering to control my
> impulse to answer her directly and to ask instead, "Should I answer
> you?" [p. 233].

I am continually surprised that such a simple and straightforward way of
assessing what the patient needs is disregarded by many analysts who
persist in believing that the decision regarding when to disclose is a
unilateral one made by them. I have found that even the most disturbed
patients are capable of discussing what they need, even if the answer is
that they don't really know. By asking the question and letting them know
that they appear to want something from me, the doors of communication
remain open. And very often I find that they know exactly what they
need. A similar issue involves responding to the patient's request, but
then going on to say too much. Admittedly, I have made this error more
times than I care to think about. And I think it is inevitable once you
engage in disclosure. But, again, the patient quickly registers her discomfort. The patient may start shifting in her chair, break eye contact and/or
look at the clock, begin to become agitated, or show some other sign of
distress. When this happens, I note it and realize I am saying too much.
I do not need to be omniscient. I merely need to look at, and listen to,

the patient. As with all interventions, the patient's response reveals whether the analyst's behavior succeeded in facilitating the analytic process, or produced an undesirable effect in the patient. As Aron (1996) says, "The critical issue seems to be whether the analyst's interventions invite or discourage further elaboration, correction, observation, and associations from the patient" (p. 98).

The alternative to directly asking the analyst a question about what he is feeling entails the use of projective identification, which has become an increasingly controversial topic that I discuss in more detail in the next chapter. Suffice it to say that I believe both therapist and patient can, and do, communicate split-off affects to each other. The receipt of these unwanted affective states can be recognized through the repetitive experience of intense, deep, and ego-dystonic emotions. Either person needs to express these felt emotions if they recur with regularity. Failing to disclose such intense and repetitive feelings often results in stalemate, and/or the patient upping the ante by becoming increasingly provocative, which I explore in more depth in the next chapter.

As I stated previously, the communication of affect is critical to the change process, and it does not seem possible to express adequately affective states without self-disclosure. Yes, the patient can observe facial expressions, note changes in voice inflection and body language. Certainly generations of analytic patients have had to make do with this limited access to the analyst's feelings. But I continually make the point that this was much easier to accomplish when patients came four, five, even six times a week. And neurotic patients are more capable of making do with the subtle emotional displays that are not verbalized by the therapist. One of the most frequent errors people make in disclosing the countertransference is by simply stating what they are feeling in a manner that is devoid of emotion. Disclosures of anger, joy, frustration, envy, love, and other intense feelings, will be rendered useless if the stated feeling is not conveyed in the verbal communication. A lifeless disclosure will only alienate or enrage the patient who needs to know and *feel* the analyst's emotional state.

Patients seeking the expression of their own disavowed affect by the therapist, those needing validation for their observations of the therapist's affective state, and those needing to engage in enactment simply cannot make do without the verbal expression of feeling by the analyst.

Renik (1995)notes that all the cautions in the literature about self-dis-closure "do not offer us very much direction with respect to everyday practical clinical choices about what to tell our patients" (p. 482).

Misuses of Self-Disclosure

Having stated that self-disclosure is an extremely valuable and underused tool in the therapist's repertoire, perhaps this point can be heightened by discussing when I think disclosure is *harmful*. The critical variables involved in a therapeutic use of disclosure are: (1) Does the patient need it, that is, does it further the process? and (2) Is it done in a way that is constructive and that the patient can use? Conversely, the hallmarks of a misuse of self-disclosure involve using it primarily to further the analyst's personal or professional agenda; or involve a well-timed disclosure that is poorly executed and fails to be therapeutic on this basis. Examples of disclosures that I consider to be misuses in most instances include: seductive disclosures of love or sexual attraction by the therapist, which necessarily means that the patient was *not* seeking this information; unsolicited expressions of the therapist's feelings of inadequacy, particu-larly when paired with idealizing comments about the patient; attempting to express intense feelings when the analyst is feeling out of control; and giving in and masochistically submitting to a sadistic patient who is demanding love or some indulgence (this necessarily requires the thera-pist to be emotionally *dishonest*, thus defeating the whole purpose of disclosure).

Here are some clinical examples of these misuses of self-disclosure. The following examples illustrate the instances cited above.

A number of years ago I was treating a young woman who was probably the most lovable person I ever saw. She was full of feeling, was emotionally available, worked hard during her sessions, and came to each session with insights and comments from the previous one. She was the kind of patient we all dream of having. Yet she had felt unloved by her mother. One day, she was crying in a heartbreaking way, telling me she felt that no one really loved her for who she was. I could not bear her pain any longer and blurted out, "But I love you." She stopped dead and was clearly shocked and startled—almost frightened. In that instant I knew I had made a terrible mistake, my disclosure being based on not being able to tolerate her pain rather than on something she needed. We both recovered from this incident, and she continued to express her deep feelings to me, but I lost some credibility that day, having completely derailed her from what she needed to explore. I might add that she was also overstimulated by my response, since she had very deep feelings toward me that frightened her and made her wonder about her sexual orientation. (She had recently married and had her first child.)

Expressing feelings of inadequacy when they are *not* being solicited can be as deleterious to the treatment as failing to disclose an error or weakness when the patient has pointed it out. Dr. W was a middle-aged analyst who prided herself on being familiar with the current analytic literature, but also felt that her years of medical education had left her ignorant in the humanities. She envied her patients who were artistic or well-versed in literature. While treating a young female patient, Nora, she was intimidated by her repeated references to literature and mythology. One day she said to Nora, unsolicited, that she admired her knowledge and also believed that Nora was significantly more intelligent than she was. Unsurprisingly, Nora left that session feeling highly anxious, and devoted many of the following hours to convincing Dr. W that she was just as intelligent as she was. Once again, we see an inappropriate disclosure is made to relieve the analyst's distress, rather than the patient's, and is unsolicited by the patient.

The most public and easily identifiable instance of giving over masochistically to a difficult and demanding patient is the case of Ferenczi and RN (Maroda, 1998). Ferenczi acknowledged in his diary that he had given in on too many fronts to RN, not realizing that what she really needed was an honest emotional response from him. For a long time he had given in to her demands for fee reductions, going to see her at her quarters, touching her, and seeing her several times a day. On the issue of the analyst going against what he is really feeling and placating a patient, either emotionally or with some other indulgence, I do not believe that this can ever be therapeutic. If you believe, as I do, that the heart of the therapeutic process is an honest emotional exchange, then any form of placation can only be destructive to the treatment.

I share the frequently-stated fear that self-disclosing analysts will say too much. But I think it is just another area where we will inevitably make mistakes from time to time. I probably make the mistake of saying too much almost every day, just as I make the mistake of withholding too much. Sometimes I am silent when I should talk , or talk when I should be silent. What determines these lapses in empathy varies from fatigue, to misunderstanding, to a need to distance, to a need to dominate or be passive, etc. Every patient wants something different, which is sometimes dizzying. And some days I just don't have it in me. Other days I surprise myself with how "on" I am, and thank God there are some of these really good days to make up for the bad ones. What makes the struggle easier is the knowledge that I will never "win"—will never achieve perfection. If I am lucky and work hard, I will be "good enough."

I also want to emphasize how important it is for the analyst to be reasonably in control of her feelings when disclosing them to the patient. Since most patients who require disclosure of intense feelings on a regular basis have problems in affective regulation, often accompanied by fears of destroying themselves or others, an out-of-control analyst fails to model the desired level of affect regulation and may terrify the patient. I have found myself yelling at particularly abusive patients in a couple of instances, and noticed the fear that quickly comes over them. If I am too angry, the patient is likely to fear that I want to get rid of her, and may become obsessed with fears of abandonment. If I know that I am over-stimulated at a particular moment in time and am likely to come on too strongly, I will contain myself and save my emotional reactions for another day when I can use them more constructively. If the patient notes that I seem to be sitting on strong feelings, I admit that I am, but also that I am having a bad day and am not prepared to deal with my feelings effectively at the moment.

In summary, I would like to reiterate that it is not necessary for the analyst to be all-knowing and all-inclusive when self-disclosing. Nor does the analyst have to be pathology-free. Certainly our capacity for correct interpretation is not flawless, nor is our capacity for empathy and under-standing. It is not sufficient, or logical, to argue against a clinical inter-vention because it cannot be executed without distortion or error.

Though some of us may shrink at this reality, most of our patients are well aware of our limitations and imperfections. We only risk closing off their experience, and their spontaneous affective responses to us, if we present ourselves in an authoritarian, bullying way. Or if we become, and remain, defensively closed off to acknowledging their experiences of us, especially once they have spotted our inevitable neuroses and character flaws.

We naturally will not agree on what is happening in the analytic relationship at all times. Sometimes we will have no choice but agreeing to disagree—or to admit to being unaware of the feelings or motivations the patient assigns to us. The willingness to consider that the patient *might* be aware of something in us that we are not is certainly not a new idea, let alone an impossible one to accept.

At other times we will have to own up to idiosyncratic responses based on our past experience, to negative feelings toward the patient, and to pettiness, greed, envy, or some other less-than-desirable trait. This will no doubt be painful and difficult for us, and may force us to change as the patient changes. We will no longer be able to hide behind our blank screens like priests in the confessional.

As to the notion that every time we reveal something, we will also be hiding something else, I have only one response: of course. This is inevitably true of us, as it is of our patients. But we also know that when we choose to *interpret* something, we are choosing *not* to interpret something else. (A point made many times by Renik and others.) And this often has as much or more to do with us than it does with the patient. We cannot escape our subjectivity nor our fallibility, but these are not reasons to reject the concept of self-disclosure.

The key ingredients to successful disclosures center on affective responses and on the therapist's willingness to be open about his or her own experience. Even if only a partial truth is revealed, or if the analyst is denying something about his own experience that the patient perceives, *it is the therapist's willingness to be forthcoming and to show emotion that is curative and stimulates emotional honesty in the patient.* If we had to be all-knowing and without pathology or weakness, few of us would be in a position to treat anyone. If we do not represent our self-disclosures as the final word, we leave room for our patients to remain skeptical if our words do not match their experience. And sometimes it will be they who enlighten us.

Chapter 5

Since Feeling Is First

Projective Identification and Countertransference Interventions

> since feeling is first
> who pays any attention
> to the syntax of things
> will never wholly kiss you
> —e. e. cummings

Projective identification cannot be discussed without first granting that it is ill-defined and often misinterpreted. Yet it holds a certain mystique for most of us who do therapy. We keep discussing and redefining projective identification because we want to truly grasp what is happening in a session when we are deeply, and perhaps suddenly, seized by an intense feeling that we were not expecting to have. We know that our affective experience is a response to the patient we are treating, but often we are uncertain about the reason for, or the origin of, our feelings. Has the patient stimulated something in us that was lying dormant, waiting to be awakened, or is he simply "depositing" his feeling in us? Is the experience of intense affect as precipitous as it often seems or is it the culmination of a series of communications between therapist and patient?

We are also curious about the patient's *intent*. Is the patient trying to communicate with us, trying to rid himself of unbearable feelings, or trying to hurt or seduce us? Is there a primary motive or is the projection of strong affect usually multi-determined? Is the patient trying to communicate with us and thereby facilitate the treatment, or is he trying to defeat us by forcing us to experience and possibly act on the most destructive feelings that he can muster? Recent discussions of projective identification focus on these questions in an attempt to solve the riddle of projective identification, as well as to formulate techniques that respond to its nature and purpose.

What follows is a brief overview of the literature on projective identification that is particularly pertinent to this discussion. The reader is referred to Scharff (1992) for an outstanding and complete review of the literature on this topic, which includes a history of its evolving changes in meaning and usage.

When Melanie Klein coined the term projective identification in 1946, she was referring to the child's fantasy of ridding himself of unwanted feelings by assigning them to someone else. This early notion of projective identification was purely intrapsychic and did not include the stimulation of feeling in another person. It was not meant to be a communication. Rather the child simply *thought* the unwanted attribute away and was able to ease her mind through this defensive act. Most current definitions of projective identification, however, focus on the treatment setting and refer to the stimulation of strong affect in the therapist. As with many psychoanalytic terms, the name remained the same, but the concept changed dramatically as it evolved from an intrapsychic to an interpersonal event. And, with this metamorphosis, the question of motivation became more complex. Originally, the only motivation was "to get rid of" an emotion. But as an event between two people, projective identification held the promise of communication. Aron (1996) notes that "Bion (1959) in particular had the greatest influence on the notion of projective identification, transforming it into an interactional construct" (p. 209), in that he postulated that the analyst would feel compelled to play out a certain role.

In 1966, Malin and Grotstein introduced the notion of normalcy with regard to projective identification, citing it as a part of the growth process in everyone. According to them, all children project onto their parents the feelings that they cannot yet manage. The task for the parent is to be capable of that which the child is not. That is, the parent needs "to contain" (Bion, 1959) the child's projected affect so that the child can identify with the parent and internalize this activity. Malin and Grotstein point out that the child is then ready to move on to higher levels of functioning, which will undoubtedly involve repeated instances of projective identification, offering the child the opportunity to use the adult as a sort of conduit for achieving affective mastery. In accordance with their view of projective identification, adults who have not accepted and integrated their own affective experience continue to use projective identification to manage their unacceptable emotions. This deficit in affect integration produces "impaired affect tolerance and an inability to use affects as self-signals," according to Stolorow et al. (1987, p. 72).

Malin and Grotstein are well aware that being stuck in a primary mode of projective identification indicates a high level of pathology that is found mostly in psychotics and borderline and some narcissistic personality disorders. They rightly point out that the mechanism itself is normal in that it occurs naturally in children and represents an attempt at growth and development. (Of course, it can and will also be used by normal adults when they are overwhelmed by their own affective experiences.) It becomes pathological when someone reaches adulthood without having attained a reasonable degree of success in integrating his affect. And, if this person enters therapy, he will bring the full force and power of an adult mind and a lifetime of repressed aggression to bear on the therapist. But the interaction will now be between patient and therapist rather than child and adult. And coping with a patient who relies heavily on splitting and projective identification is certainly not child's play.

Tansey and Burke (1989) echo the views expressed by Malin and Grotstein, and outline a step-by-step program for therapists that emphasizes the communicative and constructive aspects of projective identification. They encourage therapists to see their patients as unconsciously trying to communicate split-off affect. Therapists should be empathic both toward the patient and themselves, as they will inevitably experience strong countertransference reactions to their patients that are likely to be unpleasant and difficult. Tansey and Burke advise therapists to accept the projected feelings willingly, to experience the intended affect, to sort out what is coming from the patient (as contrasted with what is idiosyncratic to the therapist) and, finally, to use the insights to make enlightening interpretations. They caution against disclosing the countertransference, advising "silent use" of it for the purpose of guiding interpretations. This, incidentally, is a position widely supported by those who write about projective identification.

Ogden (1982) sees projective identification both as a form of communication and a form of defense. He believes that it is a genuine challenge for therapists to contain and respond to projective identifications, and notes how often treatments fail because of a therapist's inability to cope with the feelings that are stimulated in him:

> Failure to adequately process a projective identification is reflected in the therapist's response in one of two ways: either by his mounting a rigid defense against awareness of the feelings engendered, or allowing the feeling or the defense against it to be translated into action [p. 32].

Ogden's examples of the therapist "translating into action" include socializing with the patient, giving or receiving gifts, and breaching confidentiality. He acknowledges that interpretation is often unproductive, and advises therapists to be tolerant and understanding when a patient is functioning at a pre-verbal level. His only suggestion regarding technique with such patients is as follows:

> Under such circumstances, the therapist must rely on noninterpretive interventions and management of the therapy to convey his silently formulated understandings of that which the patient has unconsciously asked him to both contain and return to him in a form that he can utilize [p. 74].

Grinberg (1979) was one of the early writers on the link between projective identification and countertransference but, unfortunately—at least to my way of thinking—he views projective identification *and the therapist's response to it* as being a function primarily of the patient. Calling the therapist's response "projective counteridentification," he describes the therapist as a passive recipient of the projective identification which is "projected, lodged, or forced" into him. Grinberg views projective identification as a rather malignant process that threatens to destroy the treatment. As he says:

> One might say that what was projected, by means of the psycho-pathic modality of projective identification, operates within the object as a parasitic superego which omnipotently induces the analyst's ego to act or feel what the patient wanted him to act or feel in his unconscious fantasy [p. 180].

Like many of his analytic colleagues, Grinberg believes that interpretation of the patient's wish to have the therapist feel what he feels is the technique of choice when confronted with projective identification.

Kernberg (1987) says that projective identification is a primitive defensive operation "based on an ego structure centered on splitting as its essential defense" (p. 798). He differentiates between projection and projective identification on the basis of affective stimulation in the therapist: only projective identification produces affect in the therapist. While not seeking to pursue the varied views concerning the differences that may or may not exist between projection and projective identification, my use of the term projective identification is similar to Kernberg's, referring only to those times when intense, unexplained, and ego-dystonic affect is stimulated, usually repeatedly, in the therapist. Kernberg is quick to recognize that interventions other than interpretation are often required when dealing with the patient's projective identifications, but he also cautions therapists against "countertransference acting-out." Although he is vague about what therapists should use instead of interpretation, he is very clear about why interpretation often fails. He says, "The patient typically resists the analyst's efforts at interpretation because of the dread of what had to be projected in the first place" (p. 801)—a point that might seem obvious, yet is rarely made. Logically, those patients who are able to accept and acknowledge interpretations regarding projective identification are on the verge of knowing and accepting the feelings that were formerly split off.

But what about the patient who is far from ready cognitively to recognize and accept the split-off emotions? What is the therapist to do?

It seems to me that the whole transference-countertransference mess that often follows a projective identification is made all the worse by therapists who insist on beating their beleaguered patients over the head with interpretations they are convinced are correct. And, as the patient becomes increasingly agitated and unreceptive to these interpretations (even when they are correct), some therapists end up compounding their error: they insist that the patient is resisting their interpretations, which is no doubt due to a desire on the part of the patient to defeat the therapist and ruin the treatment.

Following along this line of thought, Finnell (1986) believes that the term projective identification is often used by therapists to avoid responsibility for their own countertransference reactions. Rather than owning up to their feelings in response to an admittedly difficult patient, some therapists are fond of speaking of their patients, à la Grinberg, as malevolent souls who force experiences of hopelessness, despair, lust, and rage down their therapists' throats. Objecting to this tendency to "dump" on the patient, Finnell says this:

> The interaction between two personalities communicating on a projective-introjective level is open to many different influences. No two analysts will react identically to the same patient. . . . I believe it is an oversimplification to propose that *any* therapist would react identically to a particular patient. Neat theoretical conceptualizations may satisfy the analyst's need for intellectualized closure, but the richness and nuances of the therapeutic interaction are lost. The ultimate value of a clinical concept lies in the degree to which it fosters accurate understanding and analytic skill. Projective identification runs the risk of shutting down rather than opening up the therapist's attitude to the patient and the clinical material [p. 106].

In his discussion of Finnell's ideas, Whipple (1986) considers the concept of projective identification to be too useful to discard. But he admits that it is often used to exonerate the analyst: it helps him to avoid the real issue of countertransference and, perhaps even more importantly, the patient can be blamed for the therapist's untoward reactions.

It seems to me that all of the above authors make good points, but I agree with Whipple when he says that it does not make sense to throw the term out because it has been used defensively in the past. Getting rid of the term projective identification will not stop therapists from being defensive, nor will it stop patients from trying anything they can to communicate their feelings to us. For myself, I regret that the term that is used to describe a patient's desire to communicate disavowed affect is so intellectualized, if not pejorative. Something more descriptive would be helpful (but, alas, Schaefer, 1976, and others have been making this point about psychoanalytic language for some time). Realistically, a new term is not likely to be adopted. What we *can* do, however, is focus on the function of projective identification in the interpersonal and clinical sense, as well as our response to it, instead of intellectualizing or creating new jargon (such as projective introjection, projective counteridentification, and introjective identification) to define what we think we are talking about. We can also help to discourage blaming our patients for our feelings by acknowledging that projective identification is a *mutual* event in the treatment relationship. No one is so healthy that he or she never projects a disavowed emotion. Scharff (1992) describes how projective identification works in intimate relationships and groups. Grotstein (1995) agrees and adds:

> One of the commonest examples of this world view is the universal finding of mutual projective identifications in married couples and in groups (Bion, 1961a; Grotstein, 1993a; Lachkar, 1992). We are all familiar in our clinical practices with how our patients often choose mates, friends, colleagues, etc. on the basis of an unconscious identification they arrogate to the object to represent an aspect of themselves that they either long to be reunited with or desire to disavow yet maintain contact with that disavowed part [p. 741].

After reading this quotation, it is hard to imagine how we could nod in agreement with Grotstein's observation, which I believe most of us would, and yet not apply the same human principle to ourselves. Do we not do the same, at least at times, with our spouses, friends, colleagues, and patients? It seems that the onus can be removed from the patient if we note that we are attending not only to the receipt of the patient's split-off affect, but also to signs that the patient has received our disavowed emotions as well. In both instances it behooves the therapist to understand what has taken place in order to facilitate best an understanding of the event. (One of the keys to understanding when the patient has received the analyst's projective identification comes in a rather straight-forward way. The patient, after feeling the discomforting affective state, will often say, "You know I feel strangely angry, sad, agitated, etc., and I don't know what to make of this. This is definitely *not* what I was feeling earlier in the session and I don't even know where it's coming from.")

Projective Identification as Communication

It seems safe to say that most, if not all, analytic clinicians accept the existence of the mechanism we call projective identification. It may even be safe to say that the current literature emphasizing the communicative and constructive aspects of projective identification, rather than the pathology and potential for destruction, also reflect the views of a majority of clinicians. If this is true, then most therapists believe that a patient tries to communicate disavowed affect so that his therapist can experience it, understand it, and find a way to live with it—the idea being that if the therapist can achieve this affective task, then so can the patient.

So, the problem for us as therapists is this: How do we let a patient know that his communication has been received? The challenge for the therapist is to acknowledge receipt of the patient's message in terms that the patient will understand. If he does not get our message, then the required cycle of communicated affect that begins with projective iden-tification and ideally ends with affective integration will not be complete. Failure on the therapist's part to participate in affective communication often results in frustration for the patient and renewed efforts on his part to send a new message, with the hope that the next one will be received and acknowledged. And when the patient, believing that the message has not been heard feels forced to repeat himself, subsequent messages are usually stronger and louder.

Traditionally, we have believed that most of our communications to patients should take the form of interpretation. Yet virtually everyone who writes about patients who use splitting and projective identification note that these patients cannot use an interpretation because they are typically or temporarily regressed at a pre-verbal level. Kernberg is not alone in saying that if a patient could acknowledge and discuss his disavowed affect, then he would have no need for projective identification in the first place. Ogden (1982) notes that the patient not only rejects interpretation but sometimes experiences it as "dangerous and inassimilable." Balint (1968), in his classic discussion of the "basic fault," says,

> At the Oedipal—and even at some of the so-called preoedipal levels—a proper interpretation, which makes a repressed conflict conscious and thereby resolves a resistance or undoes a split, gets the patient's free associations going again; at the level of the basic fault this does not necessarily happen. The interpretation is either experienced as interference, cruelty, unwarranted demand or unfair impingement, as a hostile act, or a sign of affection, or is felt so lifeless, in fact dead, that it has no effect at all [p. 175].

Lomas (1987) elaborates on what he calls the "limits of interpretation," noting how inadequate it is as an all-purpose intervention of choice with all patients, and calling for therapists to expand their repertoires for greater effectiveness.

If we accept that interpretation does not work well with patients who rely heavily on projective identification, or with any patient who, regardless of diagnosis, is communicating through projective identification at a particular moment in time, then how are we to let the patient know that we understand? If we believe the argument regarding the futility of using verbal interventions with a pre-verbal patient, then it seems obvious to me that the essence of our responses must also be pre-verbal.

As I do, Casement (1985) believes that projective identification is a form of affective communication, and he notes how important it is to the patient to know that the therapist has, indeed, received his affective message. What I am proposing regarding technique is that the therapist freely, yet responsibly, respond to the patient by disclosing the strong affect he is experiencing in response to that patient. I advocate such disclosure of the countertransference in response to projective identification because I believe it is the only viable method for completing the cycle of affective communication between patient and therapist. It enables the patient to experience the therapist's struggle to manage and express the affect that was too dangerous and overwhelming for the patient. It also lets the patient know that he is having a strong impact on his therapist, something that represents both a wish and a fear for the patient who is using projective identification. On one hand, he desperately needs his therapist to understand and experience his affect, both to prove to him that his therapist can do this and to confirm his impact on his therapist. On the other hand, the patient's worst fear is that he will be too dangerous and too powerful—that if the therapist actually does experience his affect then one or both of them will be destroyed.

The challenge for the therapist is to show and express feeling without losing control, something that the patient feels is impossible. This truly provides a model for identification purposes that the patient can use in life. For a patient to observe his therapist experiencing and constructively expressing his affect means that someday the patient may be able to do the same. I believe that this is what patients are looking for when they stimulate strong affects in us as their therapists. The implicit message from the patient is this: "I can't experience the full power of this emotion and function. Can you?" The fact that this resembles an affective game of "hot potato" is not lost on most therapists. Very often, the intensity of the patient's split-off affect *is* quite difficult to bear and presents a considerable challenge to the therapist. To the extent that the patient's affect stimulates existing conflicts or complimentary narcissistic vulnerabilities in the therapist, the situation becomes even more complex and difficult. (In the next chapter I will discuss what happens when both therapist and patient simultaneously stimulate disavowed affect in each other.)

Yet I am convinced from my own clinical experience that responding with an expression of countertransference affect, provided that I am reasonably in control and can be responsible with it, is the only way to intervene effectively with patients who cannot make use of interpretation. And I often find that an insight-producing interpretation eventually follows an emotional confrontation with a patient, whether it comes from me or from the patient. It is as if the affective exchange, once completed successfully, clears the heaviness and sense of oppression and hopelessness from the session. The patient, who seemed so impossible and so infantile, along with the therapist, who may have been behaving in a similar manner, are suddenly able to talk to one another once they have openly felt with each other.

I would be surprised if many of you have not experienced this, although not necessarily because it was planned. What may have happened is that you were mired down with a difficult patient who finally succeeded in provoking you, even though you were trying not to let this happen. Having had an emotional outburst toward your patient, you were worried that it might have made things worse, only to discover that it actually made things better, even if it scared the patient a little. However, you didn't like the experience of feeling overwhelmed and perhaps a bit out of control, and you may even have vowed not to let it happen again. You may have been glad to see that no damage was done—in fact, quite the opposite occurred. But you may have told yourself that you were lucky; the next time you might not be so lucky if you don't work harder at containing your feelings.

My position, of course, is that your success at such moments had nothing to do with luck but was a function of giving the patient exactly what he needed. Rather than avoiding the exchange of emotion with patients, I think that the therapist should work with his own feelings to gain control and finesse in expressing them for the patient's benefit. Though I have outlined the technique for disclosing and analyzing the countertransference elsewhere (Maroda, 1991) this is probably a good time to illustrate with an example.

Mary, a highly intelligent and enormously intense person, formed a very early and strong attachment to me. Though in her late 30s when she began her treatment, she was alone because of her inability to sustain an intimate relationship or close friendship. She was narcissistically vulnerable with borderline features. She worked at being soft-spoken and reasonable, yet was known by her friends and co-workers to be excessively critical, perfectionistically demanding, and prone to fits of hurt and rage when disappointed. She rarely expressed any deep feeling voluntarily, showing intense emotion only when she lost control.

She had been raised in a religious Catholic family and firmly believed that her sexual and aggressive feelings, as well as her desire for power, recognition, and love, were un-Christian and shameful. Forced by this upbringing to deny her own nature, she relied heavily on projective identification in her communications with everyone. I, of course, was no exception.

By the third year of a four-session-per-week analytic treatment, she had made enough progress to openly declare her love for me and her desire to have me with her forever. At this point, however, she was just beginning to take in the reality that this would never happen. Though she showed some progress in her ability to begin to face the separation that was inevitable, she came to this realization kicking and screaming. As the reality of our relationship became more apparent, I could literally observe her emotionally and physically trying to contain the hurt and rage that she was feeling. Convinced that I would reject her violently if I saw the extent of her rage, she fought to restrain it.

An extremely prolonged period of discord and unpleasantness resulted. Mary was distraught and inconsolable every day that she came to her sessions. When she entered my office she typically threw me an angry glance, then sat down and glared silently at me. Eventually she would begin talking, usually telling me how horribly unhappy her life had become and how the treatment had only made her worse. She alternated between criticizing and blaming me for her unhappiness, pitifully crying and demanding that I do something to help her. All of my attempts to be empathic and all of my interpretations fell on deaf ears. Occasionally, she would respond positively to some expression on my part of empathy, which forced her to stop accusing me of being indifferent to her. But only for a moment. She would return for her next session newly armed for combat, having successfully shrugged off the effects of the previous day's attempts at compassion and understanding.

For myself, I began to show noticeable signs of fatigue and stress. I felt I had a good grasp of what was happening, which served to protect me from insanity. Yet the constant wear and tear of Mary's meagerly disguised rage was unmistakably taking its toll. Clearly I had underestimated her capacity for unrelenting anguish. Finally, after several weeks, I began to break down. I was becoming depressed and no longer wanted to go to my office in the morning. In addition, I was developing psychosomatic symptoms. I had headaches, backaches, slept poorly, and generally didn't feel well. Mary predicted that I would eventually tire of her and end the relationship. I began to wonder how I was going to keep that prophecy from coming true. On a day when I was feeling particularly exhausted and had noticed a tender, enlarged spot on my neck, I called my internist, wondering if something wasn't really wrong. He examined me and told me that I was exhausted and needed a vacation. I said, "But what about my neck?" and he explained that I had managed to produce a knot in a major muscle that runs up the neck to support the head. And this knot had created the soreness and the headaches. For me that was the last straw. I left my internist's office telling myself that something had to change, and soon. Enough was enough.

That same afternoon I saw Mary and, not coincidentally, she began her session by saying that she was having a recurrence of a gastrointestinal problem that she had had prior to beginning treatment. Having already had two surgeries for this problem, she expressed her fear that she would again "twist her guts all up" with anguish. She demanded that I do something to insure that this didn't happen. My response was to say that, oddly enough, I had just come from seeing my doctor and that it seemed obvious to me that our relationship was making us both sick. Mary looked startled but stared at me quietly and intently. I went on to say that there was nothing really wrong with me at the present time, but that my body was certainly registering the high level of distress that I felt in relation to her. I added that this was clearly true for her as well. I let her know that I was upset and that I could take no more. With exasperation in my voice, I told her that I couldn't tolerate anymore of her criticism, demands, and despair. I also acknowledged that more than once I had responded to her by distancing to protect myself, which only fed her fears of abandonment and her rage at me for not doing enough or being available enough. I said I didn't want to distance from her, but that sometimes I couldn't help it. I could only take so much.

She then asked me why I thought all of this was happening. I told her that, frankly, she didn't seem to take "no" for an answer very well and that her realization that she would never have what she wanted from me frustrated and enraged her beyond belief. I said she didn't know how to bear this deprivation and defeat and seemed hell bent on destroying me if she couldn't have me, even if it meant destroying herself in the progress. I said that I was not going to let her continue trying to do that, and that she had to find another way of coping with her feelings. I emphasized her need to grieve and express anger as an alternative to withholding and criticizing. Mary was about to leave on vacation and responded unbelievably well to this confrontation. She said that she felt immensely relieved and was now able to leave me knowing I knew the truth about her.

This case example is quite an involved and complex one that could be discussed further at great length, but the point I want to make here is that only when I said, "That's it, I've had enough" and showed the emotion that went with those words, did I have a favorable impact on Mary. She needed me to experience and protect both of us from her self-destructive impulses. She knew she was feeling depressed, rejected, hopeless, and alone. What she couldn't know that she felt, and thus needed me to feel for her, was her hatred of herself and me and her desire to destroy this relationship that was making her feel so sick and unlovable. Rather than admit to herself and to me that she in some ways wanted to make this happen, she presented herself in such a way to me that it seemed likely that I would make it happen because I would be at my wit's end and feel I had no other choice. She needed me to express all the feelings she was having including, and especially, the wish to end the relationship precipitously for the dual purpose of ending our struggle and punishing both of us for what could not be.

Granted, my words also contained an interpretation, which is often but not always the case when I disclose the countertransference. But previous experience with Mary and other regressed patients has proven to me that interpretations are not heard by patients without first receiving an expression of my feelings toward them. As Stolorow et al. (1987) say, "the tendency for affective experiences to create a disorganized . . . self-state is seen to originate from early faulty affect attunement, *with a lack of mutual sharing and acceptance of affect states*" (p. 72, italics added). I believe that an essential aspect of the patient's need for an expression of the therapist's affect is related to her unheeded desire to be heard and responded to by her parents. I have never treated a patient who frequently used projective identification who did not basically feel powerless to have an emotional impact on others. Convinced of their powerlessness, such patients often project this experience onto their therapists, but with the secret hope that the therapist will prove them wrong by responding with strong feeling. Since I believe that this knowledge of interpersonal power and strength is so important, I do not share the concern that many people have about the therapist's idiosyncrasies and pathology. My feeling is that the therapist has a duty to take responsibility for his own feelings in the interpersonal therapeutic setting and, if it is done well, a little pathology will not ruin things. No one in the patient's world will ever meet the ideal of mental health and I think it is a ridiculous and unnecessary standard for therapists to expect themselves capable of maintaining it. Rather, I think we have a responsibility to maintain the therapeutic boundaries and to be as honest as we can with our patients and ourselves, particularly as it concerns our limitations.

As a last note on the need for the therapist's emotional expression in response to the patient's projective identifications, I would like to quote Grotstein (1981), someone I admire for his willingness to be dramatic and even poetic in his description of the analytic situation. In explaining *why* the patient needs to know he has succeeded in stimulating feeling, he says,

> There are certain feelings which are so constructed that they seem to be beyond words and may, therefore, have been before words were first experienced. Powerful feelings are more often than not expressed by giving another person the experience of how one feels. Throughout the course of human history, dialogue and confession seem to have been the dominant forms of emotional release. All human beings seem to have the need to be shriven, that is, to be relieved of the burden of unknown, unknowable feelings by being able to express them, literally as well as figuratively into the flesh . . . of the other so that this other person can know how one felt. The sadist and murderer desire to see the look of agony on their victim's face so as to be sure that the murderer's own tortured experience can be transmitted through the network of projective identification to the victim whose agonized face completes the communication . . . How else can a beleaguered patient know that his analyst understands than if he suffers the experience which the patient lacks the words to describe [p. 202]?

Though it is not an easy thing to do, especially when we know that our patients *want* us to be in pain, I believe that the most therapeutic act is one of surrendering to the emotional experience that they want us to have. Grotstein (1995) notes that handling all of these painful feelings can be enormously difficult, yet seems inevitable. To help our patients who cannot bear what is inside them, it is likely that we have no recourse other than to bear it for them, letting them know how and why it is

↳ but not in same way —

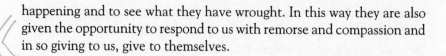

happening and to see what they have wrought. In this way they are also given the opportunity to respond to us with remorse and compassion and in so giving to us, give to themselves.

Chapter 6

Enactment
When the Patient's and Analyst's Pasts Converge

Continuing the examination of the analytic relationship as relational, mutual, and affective, we turn our attention to a critical transference–countertransference phenomenon: enactment. Formerly known as "acting out," or "acting in," we struggle to formulate a meaningful definition of enactment that does justice to the complexities of this unique transference-countertransference interplay. Many authors (Aron, 1991, 1996; Chused, 1991, 1997; Gabbard, 1995; Hirsch, 1993, 1994; Hirsch and Roth, 1995; Jacobs, 1986; McLaughlin, 1991; Mitchell, 1988; Renik, 1993; Richards, Bachant, and Lynch, 1997; Sandler, 1976) agree that enactment occurs unconsciously, that is, as an unwitting or inadvertent event on the analyst's part. The problem facing modern psychoanalysis regarding enactment is threefold. One, how do we adequately define enactment, that is, what are its critical characteristics—motivation, emotion, behavior, or some combination? Two, what are the dangers of enactment and how can we minimize them? And three, since enactment is inevitable, how can we maximize its therapeutic potential?

Defining Enactment

Chused (1991) echoes Sandler's (1976) early definition of enactment
when she says, "Enactments occur when an attempt to actualize a
transference fantasy elicits a countertransference reaction" (p. 29). Here
the enactment's point of origin lies within the psyche of the patient.
Chused views enactment as the patient's attempt to recreate the past and
gain gratification, which accounts for her belief that enactment is coun-
terproductive. In another work (1997) Chused goes as far as saying that
the therapeutic moment occurs when the analyst thwarts an enactment
and provides a correct interpretation instead.

In Chused's view of enactment the patient clearly initiates and the
analyst participates only as a response to the patient's stimulus. However,
she concedes that the APA Panel (1992) on enactment, following
disagreement as to the role of analyst and patient, concluded that
enactment is "a *jointly created interaction*, fueled by unconscious psychic
forces in both patient and analyst" (p. 265), a perspective that I share.

Hirsch (1994) definitively sees enactment as both inevitable and
therapeutic, as does Renik (1993). He defines enactment as "a living out
of affective experience, usually by both parties in the analytic dyad, within
the strict boundaries of the analytic frame" (p. 172).

Gabbard (1995) notes the confusion that sometimes arises concerning
the difference between mutual projective identification and enactment.
Since mutual projective identification refers only to the mutual stimulation of repressed, intense affect, I think Gabbard is quite right in his
distinction between the two. Although projective identification may
inspire or inform behavior, by definition, it only requires the presence of
strongly felt emotion. Gabbard notes that enactment "implies an action,"
a point also made by Hirsch.

Most definitions of enactment, then, contain these two essential
elements: the stimulation of strong, unconscious affect and some resulting behavior. Following this logical progression, a likely hypothesis states
that enactment is necessarily preceded by mutual projective identification. You could say that the mutual stimulation of repressed affect is
essentially the fuel for the engine of the behavioral event labeled as
enactment. (See Aron, 1996, for a thorough historical overview of

enactment as an analytic concept, particularly the reluctance to acknowledge the contributions of the interpersonalists.)

Richards et al. (1997) notes that enactment may take any form; that
it may be expressed through silence, action or gesture, all of which qualify
as observable behaviors. The defining characteristic of enactment, since
virtually any behavior may qualify, rests on the presence of several
essential elements. Richards attempts to define enactment by saying,

> It is characteristic of an enactment that the analyst is not aware of
> his participation as it is happening. Only after the fact does the
> analyst become aware that he has acted in a manner that goes
> against his usual grain, and is a departure from the normal course
> of communication and behavior, discourse and relationship, of the
> analytic process [p. 15].

Once again, we see that enactment is universally defined as spontaneous, difficult if not impossible to control, unconscious, and affectively
driven. Whether you believe that the analysand initiates the enactment
(as Chused and Richards do) or that either party may be the initiator (as
Hirsch, Renik, myself, and others do), who "started it" is probably
impossible to determine and does not negate the consensus that enactment is a mutual event.

Enactment differs from other strong transference-countertransference
interplays in that it is necessarily unconsciously motivated by the mutual
stimulation of strong affect, with both persons usually stating that they
felt out of control, or at least felt something come over them that was
mysterious and powerful. Behaviorally, it may take the form of a heated
argument, a sadomasochistic exchange, a spontaneous hug or other
physical gesture, a shortening or lengthening of a session, a failure to
collect the fees, an unexpected dissolution into tears, or a withdrawal
into silent rejection.

Building on the work of those cited here, I would like to expand the
definition of enactment beyond my earlier statement regarding the
necessity of a mutual projective identification preceding an enactment.
I think the concept of enactment makes more sense, and serves to

delineate the event more sharply from other affect-driven encounters between analyst and patient, if we take the existing definition further. It is not exclusively an affectively driven, unconscious, mutually acted-on set of behaviors. *Enactment is an affectively driven repetition of converging emotional scenarios from the patient's and the analyst's lives. It is not merely an affectively-driven set of behaviors, it is neccesarily a repetition of past events that have been buried in the unconscious due to associated unmanageable or unwanted emotion.*

Although we might prefer to believe that the enacted scenario is properly the patient's, it seems more likely that the enactment behaviors actually constitute an acted-out mutual scenario from both the analyst's and patient's pasts. Either party may initiate the enactment, but I would agree with those who would say that ideally the analyst's role would be a supporting one, not a starring one. This drama rightly belongs to the patient. It is his chance to relive the past, from an affective standpoint, with a new opportunity for awareness and integration.

The analyst's affective participation must be real, or the patient could not continue. The patient must be able to stimulate something in the analyst that is equally primitive and split off, so that they can relive the drama in a real way together. Enactment thus involves mutual stimulations of repressed affective experience, ideally with the patient taking the lead. Mitchell (1988) said,

> The analyst discovers himself a co-actor in a passionate drama involving love and hate, sexuality and murder, intrusion and abandonment, victims and executioners. Whichever path he chooses, he falls into one of the patient's predesigned categories and is experienced by the patient in that way [p. 295].

If we acknowledge that the analyst can only truly "fall into" this drama when she is personally touched at a deep, unconscious level, when the analyst is stimulated to re-experience some portion of her own personal drama, then we have enactment. I think this split off quality accounts for Richards's description, which states that the analyst is typically quite surprised at her own behavior and finds it to be uncharacteristic of her. Formerly this was accounted for by claiming that the patient "forced" some feeling into the analyst. But did the patient then "force" the analyst to behave in some way that was ego-dystonic and uncharacteristic? Hardly.

The analyst's feelings and subsequent behavior shock her because she does not know this part of herself. She buried it long ago, and now this patient is threatening her by stimulating something in herself that she does not want to see.

Regardless of who has initiated the enactment, it obviously has potency and therapeutic relevance only if it is mutual. If one side drops the ball and does not participate, no enactment occurs. In fact, one could argue that a major factor in a good analytic match is the ability of the analyst and patient to stimulate a therapeutic level of enactment between them, along with the ability to work through the accompanying strong affects. Too little enactment leads to stagnation; too much leads to premature termination, impasse or unacceptable acting out (repeated sadistic encounters, sexual acting out, etc.)

The Dangers of Enactment

This definition, that enactment contains an element of uncontrolled unconscious impulses that are mutually stimulated between analyst and patient, brings us to the heart of the controversy surrounding it. Although Chused (1997) says that if there was an option to enact or not enact, we would be better off if we did not (I obviously disagree), there is a consensus that enactment is inevitable. The question remains, however, what action on the analyst's part is therapeutic? And herein lies the controversy. Addressing the dangers of enactment, Chused says,

> Through my experience with the power of transference, the fervor with which patients maintain their psychic reality and actualize fantasies even without the analyst's behavioral participation (Boesky, 1982), I have learned there is no guarantee that the patient will understand an analyst's participation in an enactment, experientially, as the analyst does. Enactments are complex phenomena, with the power to inform as well as the power to impede an analysis. Neither Hirsch nor Renik seem to appreciate this complexity.

Hirsch seems to believe in an enactment for what it reflects in the analyst (the myth of the omniscient patient) [p. 271].

Richards et al. (1997) share Chused's concerns regarding the impact of enactments on the patient. He says,

> Enactments, like transference actualizations and acting-out, can serve to advance the therapeutic process or to derail it. This fact is often lost. . . . I stress all this because there is of late a tendency for the concept of enactment to be valorized in discussions of the therapeutic process [p. 7].

He goes on to ponder the possibilities for the countertransference dominating the process. This comment by Richards is the first I have found referring to the countertransference as a potential dominant force since my own mention of it in an earlier work (Maroda, 1991). There is no serious discussion in the analytic literature of the potential for the *analyst's past, rather than the patient's, being re-enacted to the point of dominating the treatment, and even determining its outcome.* Prior unrealistic expectations for the analyst's personal analysis is no doubt largely responsible for this oversight. How can the analyst possibly pollute the treatment in this way if she has already been "cured"? Somehow, even analysts who are aware of the inevitability of countertransference and of the patient's pressure to re-create the past, neglect the fact that an analyst in the throes of a strong countertransference is under the influence of the same type of repetition compulsion as the patient—and has the power in the relationship to insure that her reality prevails.

It seems not only possible, but highly likely, that when a powerful enactment between patient and analyst is not correctly identified and worked through, the patient's reality will be subjugated to the analyst's, resulting in countertransference dominance. Exactly how damaging this may be to the patient depends on many factors. These include: when the countertransference dominance develops in the treatment and how long it persists; the extent to which the transference-countertransference conflicts are resolved during the ensuing enactments; the degree to which the patient blames himself for therapeutic limitations or failures; the overall vulnerability of the patient; and the quality of the analyst's past experience in terms of its destructiveness. Analysts with less-than-average pathology and trauma in their backgrounds naturally have less that is seriously destructive to impose on their patients. However, this does not mean that harm will not be done by a relatively "healthy" analyst in cases where the countertransference dominates. Any significant diminution of the patient's experience caused by the analyst's need to replay her own past constitutes injury and a disservice to the patient, as well as a treatment failure.

Countertransference dominance also harms the analyst, who undoubtedly knows on an unconscious level that re-enactment of her past unduly influences a patient's treatment. Such an analyst is likely to be plagued with guilt and uneasiness over how a countertransference-dominated treatment is proceeding. Since such treatments are usually characterized by excessive pleasure and gratification for the analyst, by excessive conflict and defensiveness on the part of the analyst, or by some pattern of alternating between the two, I think it is impossible for the analyst not to be haunted by an awareness that things are not as they should be. Unfortunately, it can be easy to dismiss this recurring discomfort as either neurotic or as an understandable degree of distress incurred in treating a difficult patient. Countertransference-dominated treatments usually have one of two basic outcomes: either a prolonged, too-blissful treatment that ultimately is so nondynamic that it quietly extinguishes itself; or, a stormy, passionate upheaval that culminates in traumatic acting out by the analyst or a precipitous termination of the treatment by either patient or analyst.

When a difficult patient leaves treatment in anger, the temptation is great to label that patient as untreatable. Hard as it might be for the analyst to say that the patient was impossible—that no one could have done better—she may be left with a nagging sense of failure and inadequacy that keeps the patient alive and present in the analyst's mind long after termination. In extreme cases of countertransference dominance, such as when an analyst engages in sexual relations with a patient, the damage to the analyst as well as to the patient is quite obvious.

The traditional ways of dealing with the countertransference, such as self-analysis, consultation, and return to personal analysis, often fail because they rely on the psyche of the analyst rather than addressing the interpersonal nature of persistent countertransference problems and the manner in which they are enacted. Only techniques that allow for constructive interaction between analyst and patient, including the appropriate expression of intense affect, offer the possibility for working through difficult, or even traumatic, enactments.

Sometimes the analyst is unaware of characterological problems that are most likely to lead to significant countertransference dominance. Building on the contributions of Miller (1981) and Kohut (1971, 1977), Finell (1985) documented the narcissistic problems of the analyst. She discussed the unique opportunities for narcissistic gratification that exist in the analytic situation, describing how both patient and analyst can collude and deny that such gratification is taking place in the treatment setting. Although Finell did not postulate the dominance of the analyst's pathology, she did acknowledge the potential for the harm that can be done by the analyst with unresolved narcissistic issues:

> The impossibility of processing denied and split-off feelings throws the burden of responsibility on to the analyst's personal analysis. If this fails to work through grandiosity, exhibitionism, aggression, and power, the potential for countertransference over and above a specific reaction to a narcissistic transference in patients is enormous [p. 443].

Tower (1956) also noted how impossible it is for any analyst to control her own countertransference. Classical discussions of the countertransference, she said,

> presuppose an ability in the analyst consciously to *control* his own unconscious. Such a supposition is in violation of the basic premise of our science—namely, that human beings are possessed of an unconscious which is *not* subject to conscious control, but which is (fortunately) subject to investigation through the medium of the transference (and presumably also the countertransference) neurosis [p. 225].

In another early contribution to the countertransference literature, Benedek (1953) hinted at the possibility of countertransference dominance, which occurs when the analyst attempts to defend against re-creating the past with a patient:

> [Countertransference] is the analyst's projection of an important person of his past onto his patient. . . . The patient becomes . . . the feared "castrative woman" in the analyst's life, or he may become any person toward whom the therapist once felt helpless. Thus the patient, not only by the actual obligation, but also through the countertransference, becomes a partial representative of the therapist's superego; and then his inhibition in regard to that patient may grow beyond his control [p. 206].

Benedek's statement illustrates that what we know to be true of our patients—that is, the harder they defend against awareness of their own unconscious or a repetition of their past, the more likely they are to repeat it—is also true of us. Benedek's reference to the analyst's helplessness is particularly relevant in that analysts typically, and understandably, aim for a sense of mastery and legitimate control in the analytic situation. Yet one need not look far to know how easily this desire for mastery can be transformed into a defense against the feelings of helplessness that patients can stimulate. This defense then serves to block awareness of the origin and meaning of the analysts's feelings of helplessness.

Racker (1968) was also aware of the possibility of countertransference dominance, but his discussion of "neurotic countertransference" was vague in terms of how this might be played out in the treatment and affect its outcome:

> A special danger involved in neurotic countertransference is what might be called *countertransference induction* or *countertransference grafting*. By this, I mean the well-known danger of the analyst's "inducing" or "grafting" his own neurosis upon the patient [p. 125].

It is indeed frightening to consider how much self-destructive behavior, including suicide, may actually be subtly encouraged or invited as a result of countertransference dominance. Although repetition of the patient's past, up to and including the same undesirable outcome, has long been considered by many as the worst possible occurrence in treatment, I do not agree. Patients are well-accustomed to reliving their pasts, as are we all. Thus they are generally able to cope with this familiar event, no matter how painful.

However, when countertransference enactments pervade a treatment, resulting not only in inhibition of the transference but in the imposition of a significant degree of the analyst's past on the patient, it may well be traumatic. The patient may be completely unprepared for coping with an analyst's re-enactment, although this no doubt depends on the extent of shared history between patient and analyst.

An analyst who is significantly more disturbed than her patient—meaning specifically that the analyst's history includes conflicts, traumatic events, developmental arrests, or constitutional weaknesses that far exceed those of the patient—may unintentionally recreate harmful experiences that are novel to the patient and for which he has no defense. Also, countertransference dominance is more likely to occur during a period of mutual regression, which means that the patient's normal defenses would be disarmed, leaving room for serious damage.

The experience of being in control is an essential aspect of adequately defending or coping. When patients repeat the past, they do so at their own behest, and a measure of control makes the experience manageable. But when analysts re-enact their pasts with their patients, they remove control from the patient, which leads to confusion and anxiety at best and, at worst, to trauma, despair, and self-destruction.

The best example of countertransference dominance I have seen is the case of Joanne, which I first described in a previous work (Maroda, 1991). I am repeating it here because it was a consultation for referral, which leaves me freer to be non-defensive about the countertransference of the therapists involved, and because it so clearly illustrates the complexities of enactment and the potential for the analyst's past to determine the outcome of treatment.

Joanne, an attractive lesbian in her late 20s, consulted me regarding her two failed treatments. Both of her female therapists had gone to bed with her, in spite of the fact that they were both psychoanalytically trained (one was an analyst, the other was not, but both had had a personal analysis).

Joanne told me that she had abruptly fled her first treatment after she and her therapist, Dr. S, had ended up in bed fondling and kissing each other. Shortly after this incident, Joanne, suffering from an extreme anxiety reaction resulting from her sexual encounter with her therapist, was treated in a hospital emergency room by a young female psychiatrist, Dr. T.

Dr. T was sympathetic and reassuring when Joanne told her what had happened with Dr. S. Dr. T assured her that her anxiety was reasonably normal under the circumstances and concurred with Joanne that she should not return for any further therapy with Dr. S. Joanne felt very comfortable with Dr. T and asked her if she would be willing to treat her. She agreed, and the treatment proceeded well and without incident for the next 18 months. They had developed a very good rapport and formed a close attachment to each other. What happened next was therefore very disturbing to both of them.

Dr. T's husband was offered an excellent position in another part of the country, which he accepted. As a result, Dr. T informed Joanne that she would have to terminate the treatment within a few weeks. Joanne was naturally disappointed and upset, but she struggled to accept her therapist's imminent departure, understanding the circumstances. Dr. T said she was sorry to leave Joanne when her treatment was really just getting going, which helped lessen Joanne's feelings of abandonment. They continued to see each other until the week of Dr. T's departure and terminated on good terms.

Within a few weeks of Dr. T's departure, however, Joanne received a letter from Dr. T, asking that they keep in touch by mail. Joanne was overstimulated and surprised by this request, knowing it was not appropriate, but she could not refuse her therapist's offer of continued contact. They corresponded on a regular basis. One year later, Dr. T professed her love for Joanne and asked if she would be willing to see her, all expenses paid by Dr. T. Again, Joanne was reluctant because she knew this was wrong. She began to have small anxiety attacks, yet she was fascinated by her therapist's attachment to her and agreed to see her.

The relationship continued for the next two years. In the beginning Joanne was willing to fly anywhere to meet Dr. T, as they were in the throes of a love affair. (Dr. T's husband did not know about the affair, nor did Joanne's partner. Since all of them traveled frequently on business, the weekend meetings were disguised as conferences.) As time passed, Joanne became less interested in seeing Dr. T and began making excuses for failing to see her. She also wrote less and called infrequently. Joanne was feeling the stress of the affair, feeling guilty about cheating on her partner, and also experiencing anxiety and depression over her love affair with her therapist. She was frequently despondent and having increasing problems being productive at work.

Dr. T became agitated and seemingly desperate over Joanne's waning interest in maintaining the relationship. When Joanne did not return some of her phone calls, Dr. T called in great distress, demanding to know what was going on. Joanne told her that their affair was getting in the way of both her personal life and her career. She was tired of jumping whenever Dr. T called, wanting to talk or arrange to see her. Dr. T responded to this complaint by saying she was bitterly wounded. Didn't Joanne know how much she loved her? How could Joanne withdraw from her so easily and sound so cold? Dr. T finally offered to leave her husband and live anywhere Joanne desired. But Joanne begged off whenever this topic came up. Conversations of this type continued, often ending in a lovers' quarrel. During one of these quarrels Joanne ended the relationship.

Joanne sought me out for referral to another therapist, since she lived some distance from where I practiced. When Joanne presented this material she was pessimistic and discouraged. She said having an affair with her therapist was a terrible experience and one she regretted. Even though Joanne knew that both of her therapists had behaved in an unethical and irresponsible manner, she blamed herself for the traumatic sexual encounters with each of them. Joanne noted that both of these female therapists were married women with no homosexual history (she had asked and been told). Joanne could only conclude that she was at fault for her seductiveness, even though she was not the initiator of physical contact in either relationship. She desperately wanted more therapy but feared that she would only seduce her next therapist, too. (She did not feel comfortable seeking out a male therapist, feeling sure she needed a woman—but one she could not seduce.)

Joanne asked me what I thought about her situation. In interviewing her, I found her to be quite likeable, possessing an unusual degree of *joie de vivre*. Quick-witted, playful, and psychologically sophisticated, it was not difficult to imagine someone getting caught up with Joanne and her struggles. In addition to her charm, she possessed a tragic childhood history of parental loss and neglect that inspired pathos. Joanne was determined to overcome her adversity and expressed this through her intellectual and career ambitions. She seemed to inspire others to help her achieve her lofty goals.

When Joanne talked about others, however, there was more than a hint of opportunism as she spoke of dismissing people who "didn't want her to succeed." She spoke with contempt when discussing Dr. T, for whom I actually began to feel sorry as Joanne described Dr. T pitifully begging her not to leave her. In spite of Dr. T's abuse of Joanne, it was Joanne who gradually took control as the relationship progressed—so much so that it seemed debatable as to who was more traumatized by the relationship—Dr. T or Joanne. (My own reaction during these conversations with Joanne was that I ended up feeling very bad for both of them, even though I saw Dr. T as responsible for what happened and unquestionably guilty of sexual abuse of Joanne.)

As I talked more with Joanne about her relationships, there appeared a pattern of her ambivalence toward anyone to whom she was strongly attached. She tended to idealize others and later discard them with contempt, although this was not true of all her relationships. However, most of the people she kept in her life were those whom she easily dominated. Joanne had a history of problems with intimacy, having had many lovers. It seemed that whenever anyone got too close, Joanne tended to withdraw.

Regarding Joanne's enactment with Dr. T, clearly she followed her usual pattern of seduction and abandonment. Unfortunately, this relationship could not be worked out because the frame had been broken—the relationship had literally been taken out into the streets. Had they continued in therapy, I have no doubt that some version of this scenario would have taken place. Joanne was very successful in her psychological seduction of Dr. T, leaving Dr. T vulnerable to Joanne's inevitable withdrawal. Had therapy continued within the appropriate limits, this emotional situation could have been worked through. Instead, Dr. T's irresponsible behavior led to an untimely and painful ending.

Although I am not privy to all of the information I would need to discuss adequately Dr. T's role in this enactment, I did ask Joanne some questions. Naturally I asked Joanne if she had ever been molested. She said that although relations in her family had been sexually tinged, there had been no incest or molestation of any kind. Then she said, "But both of my therapists told me that *they* had been molested as children. Is that important?"

Given this startling information, it seems likely that both of Joanne's therapists were somehow re-enacting their own history of sexual abuse as a response to her. Perhaps being caught up in the pathos of Joanne's life and reliving their own painful childhood experiences became more than they could bear. (To what extent either of these women may have been suppressing or repressing a homosexual preference adds more to the drama.) Although it is impossible to determine exactly what took place in the minds of these two therapists, they clearly became over-involved with their highly intelligent, ambitious, talented, and wounded patient. They apparently denied their own vulnerability and neediness through their sexual enactment with Joanne.

After hearing how cold and rejecting Joanne could be toward these women, I imagined that both of them were frustrated and hurt by her and sought to restore magically the emotional merger they had previously enjoyed. Overstimulated and abandoned, they had taken the only route they knew to re-establish intimacy with their elusive patient. Yet they unquestionably repeated their own histories as they concluded their relationships with Joanne. In both cases the countertransference, rather than the transference, ultimately prevailed.

It is hard to know what could have happened differently to avoid the tragic consequences of the enactments that took place in both of these treatments. But given that both therapists had a history of being sexually abused, and the patient did not, it is easy to argue that the countertransference dominated and thus destroyed, both treatments.

Had both these therapists been able to acknowledge their strong identifications with Joanne, as well as their intense attachments to her, the outcomes might have been different. Had they confronted Joanne with her cold and rejecting behavior, and helped her to experience and understand her fear of abandonment, some real therapy could have taken place.

When I interviewed Joanne it was clear to me that she had no real understanding of her role in these relationships. The only sense of responsibility Joanne felt for the disastrous outcomes of her treatments revolved around grandiose visions of herself as evil, irresistible, and untreatable—all of which shored up her narcissistic, defensive structure in the service of denying her underlying vulnerability.

(Follow-up note: For those who might be thinking that Joanne was indeed untreatable, I did refer her to an analyst in her area and she was successfully treated over a period of nine years by this woman. In the follow-up conversations I had with Joanne, it was evident that this analyst was also quite taken with her, but in a much healthier way than the previous therapists. She idealized Joanne just enough to satisfy her narcissism, but was consistent, reliable, gave her good feedback and, most importantly, maintained the boundaries of the professional relationship. The resulting changes in Joanne were impressive, including an obvious reduction in her grandiosity, a more empathic and warm demeanor, and the ability to sustain an intimate relationship.)

Upon hearing about a case like Joanne's, where the therapists committed what might be considered to be the "ultimate sin," it is easy to distance and say, "I have never done anything like that and never would." As true as this may be, we all have had treatment failures that haunt us—situations where we felt too much and knew too little about how to manage it. And even our successful treatments are often marred by long stalemates motivated by the untoward inhibition of strong feelings. Frequently our fears of being out of control prevent us from working constructively with what we feel.

Therapeutic Uses of Enactment

Having described enactment as inevitable, as behavior emanating from unconscious affects and, therefore, being difficult to control, is it truly possible to manage enactment in a therapeutic manner? Doesn't the example of Joanne confirm Chused's and Richards' aforementioned fears that enactment can be dangerous? Certainly. But the point I want to make is an obvious one: any intervention can potentially go wrong, or be inherently dangerous and destructive. Enactment is a dynamic, naturally occurring manifestation of the transference and countertransference merging into a living entity, making the past alive in the present. This mix will always include some element of re-creating the analyst's past. In general, we can safely say that the goal should be that more of the patient's past be re-created than the analyst's, and even more importantly, that the patient have every opportunity to safely work through these events within the boundaries of the analytic relationship.

None of us can control how we feel, only how we behave. And even in the light of accepting that we are destined to re-create our pasts to some extent with our patients, we can still have a great deal of control over how we express ourselves in these situations. (An analyst who finds herself repeatedly unable to control her behavior should stop treating patients and seek additional personal analysis.) The difference between malpractice and successful treatment for Joanne centered not so much on her therapists' feelings toward her but rather on how those feelings were managed and expressed. Joanne told me that her final therapist was very forthcoming with her, letting her know when she was withdrawing, or being contemptuous, and how her therapist felt about it. As a result, they were able to work through these issues together. Concurrently, she let Joanne know that she cared about her and admired her, which Joanne loved once she realized that these feelings in her analyst would not lead to abuse.

Renik (1993) says that in order to appreciate the value of enactment, we must change the way we think about the therapeutic action of psychoanalysis. He makes the point that Freud, in accordance with the widely held views of his time, believed that action and introspection were mutually exclusive processes. This belief produced an untoward emphasis on thinking rather than doing. I agree with Renik that we need to develop a better appreciation of the value of acting and expressing, as part of the process of working through and understanding, rather than viewing these vital emotional expressions as alien to the analytic endeavor.

Another anachronistic view of the analytic process states that the patient in the throes of the transference distorts reality and imagines that the analyst feels toward him in the present what some other family member had felt toward him in the past. I was taught this as a young therapist and believed it. Thus, I would wisely interpret to the patient that he *thought* I felt a certain way because he had experienced this in the past.

What I began to realize after many years of clinical experience is that quite often patients would effectively stimulate in me the exact emotions they had experienced with someone else in the past. (And I would do the same with them.) What turned out to be therapeutic was the constructive expression of these deeply felt emotions, as well as the mutual working through of the subsequent emotional and behavioral events.

We are now left to determine what action on the analyst's part is most therapeutic. The reader may be under the impression that, in spite of my warnings regarding countertransference dominance, I advocate free expression on the part of the analyst. This is both true and untrue.

The inevitability of enactment says more than a little about its therapeutic potential. Anachronistic advice about trying to avoid enactments seems senseless to me. Rather than downplaying the importance of enactment, I prefer an emphasis on greater awareness of just how ubiquitous it is and on how equally inevitable is the evocation of the analyst's past *in terms of re-creating an emotional scenario.* I want to emphasize that while it necessarily involves action, enactment is essentially an affective event. The action carries the purpose of fully expressing the intense emotion at the heart of the transference-countertransference exchange.

For example, someone who was sexually abused as a child obviously does not need to be sexually abused by his analyst, but he may need to stimulate intense anger, a desire to harm, or intense sexual feelings in the analyst. The more prepared the analyst is to experience these feelings as a natural event in the treatment, the less likely the analyst is to repeat the past in a literal, and traumatizing, way.

Failing to appreciate that the emotional intensity of enactment constitutes its inevitability, rather than a particular behavior, could lead to irresponsible acts on the part of therapists. What has happened to a small degree regarding self-disclosure, the tendency of some therapists to indulge themselves at the patient's expense, may also happen once we accept the inevitability of enactment.

The experience of unconsciously stimulated strong, or even overwhelming, affect is completely out of the analyst's control and is inevitable. Her behavior is not.

Certainly one of the realistic outcomes of a personal analysis should be that the analyst is reasonably in control of how she behaves. And I say this with a full understanding of just how difficult it can be to manage intense countertransference feelings. I have felt murderous rage at patients. I have wanted to hit them. I have wanted to throw them out of my office, or even out of my office window. I have wanted to scream obscenities at them and tell them to get out and never come back. On the other side, I have wanted to make love to them, I have felt overwhelming grief upon witnessing their spontaneous heartbroken expressions and been tempted to hold and comfort them. And I have withdrawn into silence when I knew I should not. I have envied some of my patients to the point of shame. Worst of all, I have lapsed into a kind of deadness where I did not care about anything and knew the patient was aware of it. None of these feelings were within my control.

Sometimes I deny them or try to minimize them. On a bad day, I can let myself off the hook by blaming my patients for what lies in my own heart. On a good day I accept what I feel, knowing that it is useless to fight it and that I will work better as a therapist if I just allow all of my feelings to wash through me and over me. Even if I am ashamed of them. And this gives me greater control over my behavior.

Knowing that I cannot control what I feel does not in any way let me off the hook for how I behave. Analysis is, by definition, a situation where both persons mutually inhibit certain behaviors in the interest of facilitating the therapy and maintaining the appropriate boundaries. Even very regressed and emotionally-charged patients rarely act out in completely unacceptable ways. They talk about how much they would like to do it. They talk about how difficult it is to control themselves. Nonetheless, because they do not want to destroy the treatment, they usually *do* control themselves, or leave if they cannot. If our patients are capable of such restraint in the face of their most primitive fears and desires, how can we assume that analysts cannot be? Both analyst and patient know that it is incumbent upon them to control their own behaviors to the extent that the therapeutic limits are not seriously transgressed. Otherwise the treatment is over.

But within this small theater, where only certain acts can be played out, there is no such limitation on the world of emotion, which is at the heart of the therapeutic enterprise. All manner of emotions can be expressed, by both analyst and patient, even though the analyst must take greater responsibility for finding constructive and helpful ways to express herself. For example, rather than simply disclosing every strong feeling the analyst has, feelings should be expressed at the patient's direction and behest, allowing him to be in control of the emotional action between them. If the analyst discloses primarily when the patient asks for it, either overtly or through repeated projective identifications, then the patient is less likely to be victimized by the analyst's need to relieve herself at the patient's expense.

In the aforementioned case of Joanne, it seemed inevitable that all three of her therapists were destined to fall in love with her in some way, given who she was and what she stimulated. Two of these therapists succumbed to destructive acting out, while the third enjoyed her positive feelings toward the patient, and responsibly disclosed both positive and negative emotions that she experienced.

I am not saying that a good therapist is above being out of control with a given patient. Because we are human, this sometimes happens. But therapists who cannot control themselves to the point of violating the patient have no choice but to end the relationship and give the patient the opportunity to seek therapy elsewhere.

Enactment now joins the discovery of countertransference and self-disclosure as ubiquitous and inevitable events. Once again, however, we are discovering an aspect of the analytic process that has always existed. We are describing formerly ignored, partially defined, or neglected aspects of the analytic relationship. Taking steps to further our understanding necessarily leads to a greater awareness of both the dangers and the therapeutic potential of these aspects of the analytic process.

The challenge for those of us who embrace a two-person psychology is to examine, understand, and integrate these heretofore neglected aspects of the therapeutic relationship, such as self-disclosure and enactment. Many of the spokespersons for a theoretical perspective that places more of the emphasis on the patient, like Chused and Richards, wisely caution us not to become too enamored of our relational discoveries. Although I differ with them in their views of enactment and general reluctance to embrace mutuality, I strongly agree with their belief that the object of the analysis is the patient, not the analyst.

If a patient observes that I seem to have "started" an enactment that occurs between us, and I intuitively know this to be true, I will admit it—but resist the temptation to analyze the analyst. It is one thing for *me* to know and understand how I am re-creating my past; it is quite another thing to make this the focus of the treatment. Believing as I do that the therapeutic action of psychoanalysis centers on expressed affect, allows me to focus on admitting what I am feeling, and taking responsibility for it, while avoiding extensive forays into explaining my behavior. If some explanation is essential for the patient's understanding of the enactment, I try to keep it brief and return the focus to the resulting impact on the patient.

Believing that giving the patient an emotionally honest response, in the moment, is essentially therapeutic—provided that the analyst expresses herself clearly and responsibly the majority of the time—is at the heart of accepting enactment as inevitable and potentially useful. Accepting that patient and analyst are fated to move each other in mysterious and unplanned ways leaves room for accepting being both the recipient and the stimulator of intense, unexpected emotion. And this acceptance leaves further room for exploring the most therapeutic ways in which to work through the re-created scenes from the past.

Chapter 7

Therapeutic Necessity or Malpractice?
Physical Contact Reconsidered

Physical contact remains a highly controversial and emotional issue for analytic clinicians. Most of us prefer to bypass it altogether by simply explaining to our patients that we do not engage in physical contact. Our training has taught us to conceive of any physical engagement with our patients as "acting-out"—always an episode of unseemly gratification by an obviously insufficiently analyzed clinician. In the world of psychoanalysis—the ultimate verbal achievement—physical contact has carried the valence of unseemliness and exploitation, not to mention a certain vulgarity. As an intellectual pursuit, the moment of perfection in a psychoanalysis was imagined to be the perfectly-timed and executed interpretation, followed by the patient's illuminating insight. Here, mutuality consisted of two sets of mental gears shifting seamlessly together in an intellectual tour de force. Granted, the end product was supposed to be heightened self-awareness and newfound emotional integration, but the medium was clearly mind-mind, not mind-body.

Shapiro (1996) in her recent discussion of the "embodied analyst" decries the analytic view of body language as somehow inferior to that which is verbally expressed, taking issue with the notion that *everything* worth expressing can eventually be represented in language. While I agree with her basic assumption that we need to address the mind-body reality better than we have, I have one criticism of her work. Though I have no doubt that people *do* become aware of previously unconscious feelings when undergoing various forms of body work, such as deep massage, Rolfing, and varieties of physical therapy, Shapiro never makes it clear how body work can be integrated with psychoanalysis. Having made the point that the unconscious can, indeed, be made conscious through physical contact, she begs off making any recommendations on how to incorporate the physical into psychoanalysis—other than for clinicians to pay more attention to their own bodies and to their patients' bodily states.

Orange (1995) provides a facile discussion of the concept of "emotional memory." She quotes McDougall, who says "emotion is *essentially psychosomatic*," Bollas (1987), who talks about "somatic memory," and Stern (1983), who argues that affect memory is "only roughly translatable into a language code." Orange herself believes that emotional memory resides in both the mind and the body, yet like Shapiro, cannot say how this understanding can be applied to the issue of physical contact in the actual treatment situation—if it indeed can.

Since few clinicians are in the habit of saying what they actually do in their consulting rooms, it is no surprise that the literature on physical contact is amazingly sparse, and contains few clinical guidelines. Goodman and Teicher (1988) noted almost ten years ago that physical contact was highly controversial and infrequently discussed. Obviously, things have not changed much in the past decade, and physical contact remains a highly charged topic. Even though more clinicians are willing to consider that touch may be therapeutic, there remains an ethical and technical need to know how much touch is therapeutic, when it is therapeutic, and with whom it is therapeutic.

Analytic clinicians who were taught that the only appropriate physical contact was *no* physical contact are now left with the prickly decision of who to touch, how to touch them, and when to touch them, assuming the conventional wisdom was wrong and that touch is indeed therapeutic when used appropriately.

While I have not sufficiently answered these questions for myself, I have experimented with touch, read others' accounts of touching their patients, and worked hard to understand what my patients are really seeking when they ask me to touch them.

What I have found is that the request for physical contact has many different meanings, and that the answer to the question of "to touch or not to touch" lies in the adequate understanding of the patient's request and the analyst's emotional response to it. Understanding the patient's intrapsychic meaning, placing this in an appropriate historical context, understanding how the current request for touch represents a reen-actment in the transference-countertransference interplay, and then making the right decision, are exceedingly daunting tasks. They require intellectual and emotional depth on the analyst's part; a profound knowledge of the patient; and an ability to be aware of the affective countertransference, for example, "What am I feeling? Do I want to touch the patient? Am I afraid? Am I repulsed? Do I feel used or violated at the prospect of touching the patient? Am I sexually aroused?" Or even, "Do I feel the *opposite* of what the patient consciously seeks? Do I feel like hitting her instead of hugging her?"

Let me assure you that I make no claims of mastery in this area. Rather, I have some ideas about physical contact, including some clinical guide-lines based on what we presently know. This chapter includes case material from a current patient who has recently challenged me to confront my ideas about physical contact as she not only demands it, but ridicules me for my reluctance to be physical with her. This patient is very challenging on all fronts, remaining someone who makes me question everything I do, making me grow yet also making me furious. I have acquiesced in some of her demands and steadfastly refused to accede to others. So this case presents the opportunity to pursue the joint issues of when to touch and when not to touch, since I have repeatedly made both decisions in relation to this patient.

Before presenting this case, I would like to spend some time estab-lishing a historical perspective on the issue of touch and acknowledging the pertinent work of others.

First of all, it goes without saying that classical analysis has traditionally forbidden physical contact of any kind, including a handshake. Myriad articles from the past contain innumerable references to patients' attempts to make physical contact and their analysts' deft handling of the situation, turning the quest for contact into insight regarding the patients' motivations. It was, and remains, a given that child analysts are exempt from this taboo because their young patients do not possess the requisite language development or impulse control to make abstention possible.

Perhaps the most famous reports of therapeutic physical contact are those made by Ferenczi. These are epitomized in his *Diary* (Ferenczi, 1932) accounts of the treatment of his patient, Elizabeth Severn, code-named RN, a case I referred to earlier in this text. Ferenczi's frequent breaking of the taboo on physical contact with patients was largely responsible for his being rebuked by Freud and later ostracized and disgraced in the analytic community. Though his contributions and courageous experiments are now being given their due, his work was virtually ignored or maligned for more than sixty years. And, more importantly for this discussion, his use of physical contact remains the focus of his masochistic submission to RN and his own admission of an early, naive belief in a "love cure." In this context, his use of physical contact can easily be dismissed as one of his early errors and excessive indulgences.

Following Ferenczi's fall from grace, the psychoanalytic literature makes little mention of touching patients until Winnicott's (1969) reported use of physical contact with adults. His case illustration, coming some 35 years after Ferenczi's experiments, discusses physical contact with his now-famous patient, Margaret Little. In a thinly disguised report of her case, he says,

A variety of intimacies were tried out, chiefly those that belong to infant feeding and management. There were violent episodes. Eventually it came about that she and I were together with her head in my hands.

Without deliberate action on the part of either of us there developed a rocking rhythm. (He goes on to say that it was rather rapid and therefore arduous.) . . . Nevertheless, there we were with *mutuality* expressed in terms of a slight but persistent rocking movement. We were *communicating* with each other without words. This was taking place at a level of development that did not require the patient to have maturity in advance of that which she found herself possessing in the regression to dependence of the phase of her analysis [p. 258].

I have not been able to find any evidence that Winnicott's use of physical contact received much attention, either positive or negative. Like many case examples given by Searles, reports of unusual interventions with very primitive patients seem to be taken lightly as colorful exceptions.

Little (1990) herself has advocated physical contact at certain times, presumably based on her self-reported highly successful treatment experience with Winnicott. She praised him for his empathy and understanding, and for his willingness to touch her. During a difficult period in her treatment with Winnicott, when she was quite regressed and reportedly immobilized, she says,

> D.W. came to me at home—five, six, and sometimes seven days a week for ninety minutes each day for about three months. During most of those sessions I simply lay there, crying, held by him. He put no pressure on me, listened to my complaints and showed that he recognized my distress and could bear with it. As I recovered physically the depression gradually lifted, and I was able to work again [p. 52].

So we see that both Winnicott and Little report vignettes of her therapy involving physical contact, each regarding these episodes as important and therapeutic. They paint a picture of compassionate touch that seems unchallengeable. Both have agreed that it was therapeutic. Both found the moments of contact to be emotional and gratifying. Yet there is another side to the story of Little's analysis with Winnicott. Though she reports having had a far better experience with him than with her prior analysts, this was not an untroubled treatment.

Little was hospitalized on several occasions, having regressed to the point of psychotic decompensation. There was the aforementioned period when she was "unable" to leave her house and Winnicott came to her. And on one occasion Winnicott prophylactically hospitalized her as he was going on vacation, for fear she would have a breakdown while he was away, even though she was perfectly functional at the time. Just as with Ferenczi's treatment of RN, the regression to psychotic decompensation of a formerly nonpsychotic patient, leaves open the question of excessive gratification and infantalization generating malignant regression. And the presence of extensive physical contact in both cases represents a possible contributing factor to both patients' decompensations. However, we do not have enough information on either case to draw a conclusion as to whether some breakdown during regression was inevitable. We have no way of knowing whether the refusal of physical contact and other parameters would have been equally or more therapeutic. Rather, we can only review these case histories involving physical contact and hold them for consideration.

Little discussed her subsequent use of physical contact with her own patients and had this to say about it:

> I use my hands a good deal, both in gesture and in touch, in analyzing delusion, but it is not easy to convey just how, when, and why I move or touch a patient. Most often it is simply putting my hand somewhere, according to the context, as when I put my hand on Alice's ankle when she felt caught in the trap [this a reference to a previously reported case], or if there is severe headache I may put my hand on the patient's forehead [pp. 100–101].

But once again we see the reference to using touch with "delusional" patients, not patients who remain in touch with reality. Does this mean that Little never touched patients who were *not* delusional? Based on my own clinical experience, I doubt it. Her reports probably have more to do with the likelihood that any article on touching "normal" patients would not have been published. Yet, she still makes her point, which is that touch provides a stabilizing, orienting function for patients who are either losing touch with reality, or who fear such a loss of bearings.

Searles (1963) expressed concern about Little's recommendations for physical interventions, saying that he found declining to make physical contact on some occasions as therapeutic as his willingness to touch at other times. Searles's examples of therapeutic physical contact, as with Little and Winnicott, are limited to patients who are frankly psychotic or in the throes of a psychotic transference. And even in this context, there is both consensus and disagreement. Yes, sometimes physical contact is helpful, yet at other times it may not be. Balint (1968) warns us against providing too much gratification, noting that the goal is to reduce overall tension and promote understanding. Toward this end he does not prohibit physical contact, but rather points out that the "action" of psychoanalysis is more properly symbolic than literal.

Most modern references to touch involve cautionary tales or defenses of the traditional views on abstention. Casement's 1982 paper, "Some Pressures on the Analyst for Physical Contact During the Reliving of an Early Trauma," has become a classic. He joins his predecessors in noting the tendency for patients with trauma histories to clamor for physical contact. Those who know of Casement as a distinctly unclassical analyst and one who endorses "listening to the patient" might also expect him to endorse some use of touch. In the case he presents, he initially agreed to consider the patient's request for physical contact, chiefly because she declared herself unable to continue in the treatment without it. Casement then discovered he was not comfortable with the situation. His patient had said to him, "You *are* my mother and you are *not* holding me" (p. 282). (Again, we see the presence of delusional material.) He describes his conflict as follows:

> I reflected upon my dilemma. If I did *not* give in to her demands I might lose the patient, or she might really go psychotic and need to be hospitalized. If I *did* give in to her I would be colluding with her delusional perception of me, and the avoided elements of the trauma could become encapsulated as too terrible ever to confront. I felt placed in an impossible position [p. 283].

Casement resolves his dilemma by becoming aware of the projective identification at work in stimulating his own feelings of helplessness and he makes this interpretation to the patient. When she says that she wants him to feel what she feels, he replies,

> In one sense I am feeling that it is impossible to reach you just now, and yet in another sense I feel that my telling you this may be the only way I can reach you. Similarly I feel as if it could be impossible to go on, and yet I feel that the only way I can help you through

this is by my being prepared to tolerate what you are making me feel, and going on [p. 282].

The outcome was that the patient told Casement that he really understood her and she no longer asked for any physical contact. The treatment proceeded well with no repetition of the demand for touch. While I have no reason to doubt Casement's good result from *refusing* physical contact, I can't help but wish his discussion of the case had included the possibility that some other patient might actually need the physical contact in order to continue. Casement's paper has become not only a classic, but a classic defense of the use of interpretation as the only true analytic response to a request for touch.

Stewart (1989) warns against physical contact, finding in his experience that it often stimulates incestuous fear and other anxieties. Gabbard (1996) cautions against physical contact, noting that sexual boundary violations begin with nonsexual hugging, and that therapists have been found libel in cases of boundary violations, even when there has been no erotic contact.

Goodman and Teicher (1988) provide an even-handed discussion of the "touch issue." They note that the historical ban on contact no doubt serves the purpose of protecting the analyst, as well as the patient, from stirred-up primitive feelings and the desire to seek pleasure in the therapeutic relationship. They categorize touch as being either "holding" or "provoking":

> The purpose of the holding is to communicate the presence of a net of safety within the therapeutic relationship, offering assurance or reassurance, restraint, comfort. The offering is an attempt by the therapist to delimit the patient's distress, to minimize pain, or/and to protect the patient from harming himself or herself. Provocative or evocative touching is designed to surface new content not available at present to patient and therapist [p. 492].

My own experience with touching tends to fall more often into the "holding" category than into the provocative one, simply because it is a much safer position. Touch for the purpose of provoking the patient's suppressed or repressed emotions is riskier, and to my mind, usually requires that the touch be initiated by the therapist rather than the patient; I generally do not advise therapist-initiated touch.

On this issue, Goodman and Teicher report the results of an interesting doctoral dissertation done in 1982. The author of that study, Gelb, reports that six out of ten women said that nonerotic touching in their treatment was therapeutic. Gelb reported several other conditions that existed for the group reporting that touch was therapeutic:

> There were five conditions which appeared to be centrally related to the positive outcome. 1) Patient and therapist discussed the "touch event," the boundaries of the relationship, and the actual or potential sexual feelings. 2) The patient felt in control of initiating and sustaining contact. 3) Contact was not experienced as a demand or need satisfying for the therapist. 4) The overall expectations of the treatment were congruent with the patient's experience of the treatment. 5) The emotional and physical intimacy were congruent [p. 496].

By the way, the four out of ten patients in Gelb's study who found the use of touch to be *nontherapeutic* said that their therapists were not comfortable with the expression of hostility. The therapists worked at creating a warm, affectionate relationship in therapy, thereby blocking any expression of patient anger. This illustrates that touch can be used defensively to inhibit the patient's emotional expressions.

Because touch has been verboten in psychoanalysis, any use of it defensively by the analyst somehow seems worse than other forms of therapist defensiveness. Yet there is no reason for this to be true. McLaughlin (1995) has written eloquently on the traditional resistance to the therapeutic use of touch and described his personal evolution in this area of technique. He said that early in his career he stopped patients from hugging him in the belief that the outcome would be positive. To his surprise, and chagrin, what followed instead was "misery" and stalemate. Having experienced so many negative results, he decided to let patients hug him, but not to initiate hugging. (Once again, we see the emphasis on the patient initiating physical contact rather than the therapist.) And he reports very good results from this approach.

Interestingly, he credits some of his comfort with touch to his age and experience, which raises the question of whether or not neophyte

therapists could adequately handle therapeutic touch. Yet in McLaughlin's experience, which is also mine, that patients are deeply wounded
and alienated by the analyst's rejection of physical contact, is it not
necessary to provide adequate training and preparation for new therapists? McLaughlin changing his position on touch over the years probably
has as much or more to do with accumulated clinical wisdom as anything
else. Had he known what to do as a young analyst, I think it likely that
he would have risen to the occasion.

    In his writing on touch McLaughlin makes another very important
point, which is that patients may seek physical contact when the empathic connection between analyst and patient is broken. I think this is
an extremely important point to make.

    Although I do not think we should be in a position of degrading, or
totally rejecting the idea of physical contact, I do believe it should be used
sparingly. Wholesale acceptance of the patient's initiation of non-erotic
physical contact is potentially as damaging as wholesale rejection. The
essential analytic inquiry of, "why now?" applies as much to the quest for
touch as anything else.

    If the analyst's answer to this question is that he or she is preoccupied,
stressed, ill or in any way less emotionally available, there lies an opening
for addressing this issue with the patient. Again, this would not necessarily mean rejecting the spontaneous contact by the patient, but rather
inquiring about it later. An example might be, "I've noticed that you seem
to feel the need for more physical contact with me than usual. Does it
seem harder to feel connected for some reason?" Or if the analyst knows
with certainty that he or she has been unavailable, something more
straightforward would be appropriate, such as, "I know I have not been
as emotionally available lately, do you think this has something to do with
you needing to touch me more often?"

    I'd like to turn now to the patient I mentioned earlier who has
repeatedly challenged me on many fronts, not the least of which is her
fervent desire for physical contact. Susan, a 50-year-old lesbian, has been
in treatment three to four times per week for the past two years. She came
for analytic treatment after several briefer, mostly behavioral or supportive treatments, which provided symptom-relief only. When Susan came
to me at age 48 she was unemployed, without a partner, and said she was
"stuck." What this meant was that she seemed unable to motivate herself

to look for a job, even though she had been unemployed for some time and was using up all of her savings. Equally, she was quite lonely but couldn't seem to make the effort to meet people. Mostly she read, making some effort to find some company on the weekends. I responded by saying, "How long have you been this depressed?" And she looked at me with surprise.

Through most of her life Susan had been a "pull-yourself-up-by-your-bootstraps" kind of person. Any thoughts of weakness or depression, let alone decompensation, were unthinkable. She had worked hard, put herself through college, and worked her way up to an executive position at a large corporation. She prided herself on her "corporate identity" and savvy, in spite of the fact that she had not been able to stay at a job for the past eight years.

Around the age of 40, Susan seemed to begin to lose herself. She began to hate the corporate world, lost interest in her 15-year personal relationship, and soon ended both to take "some time off." She ended up going for therapy, but did so with a lesbian therapist who, after about six months, ended the treatment and started an affair with Susan. This ended after a short time, in a violent argument that began over Susan's refusal to take care of her former therapist.

From the beginning of Susan's treatment with me she was intent on having this treatment "work." She said she was running out of time and money and something had to happen so she could get "unstuck." As the treatment proceeded Susan purchased and read books on psychoanalysis with a vengeance. She did so out of genuine interest in the subject matter, but also out of a desire to manage her own treatment. She was determined not to be taken advantage of or shortchanged this time. She regularly tested my knowledge by bringing up psychoanalytic references and asking me if I was familiar with them. Naturally, she also read my publications, including my book on countertransference.

As the treatment progressed she began to understand how superficial her previous treatments had been, and how much there was to understand. She slowly began to take in that her "perfect parents" had done irreparable damage through their insistence that she never cry or show any strong emotion. She described her childhood as a continuous power struggle between herself and her parents. Being called out of bed in the middle of the night to re-wash the dishes, or being forced to come home from school in the middle of the day because her bed was not made properly were not uncommon occurrences. Her parents demanded an apology for each of these "infractions." Unlike her three younger siblings, Susan usually refused.

Her parents' response to this was to throw her down on the floor, or up against the wall—often slapping or almost choking her. All she had to do was say she was sorry. But she would not. Frequently she was thrown into the basement to contemplate her disrespectful attitude—sometimes spending the night sleeping on a pile of damp, dirty laundry. A couple of times her mother drove her to a nearby orphanage and ordered her to get out of the car, even though she was only a young child.

Her parents were respected pillars of the small community in which they lived and she was told by them that what they did was "for her own good"—which she believed. As a result, Susan has been a very controlled, but pleasant and even charming person throughout her life. She prides herself on her ability to mingle well and never thought much about the fact that she is emotionally constrained to the point of being unable to name any feeling other than anger.

But as we began talking about her childhood, with me noting that what her parents had done was cruel and gratuitous, she was overcome with emotion. Just when I expected that she would break down sobbing, something else happened. Susan, who was using the couch, started twitching and began letting out gasps of air, like someone who was suffocating. I asked her what was happening. What was she feeling? But she responded by becoming more physically agitated, sometimes sitting up and looking at me with wild, pleading eyes. She could not say anything meaningful about what she was feeling, and she could not cry. The first time this happened, the session ended with no real understanding on either of our parts as to what exactly was happening. Susan got up from the couch as she tried to compose herself. But she kept gasping, looked like she was going to collapse physically, and gave me that same wild-eyed look that can only be described as the look of an animal caught in a trap. Just as she was about to leave she jerkily moved forward and grabbed my hand. I let her take it, but I felt frightened both by her demeanor and the suddenness of her action. My startled response was not lost on her, and came up during the next session, which was the following Monday.

Susan told me that she was surprised by the level of feeling she experienced in her session—that this was something quite new to her. But she also added that she felt my discomfort when she took my hand, almost as though I was frightened. She said this hurt her feelings very much and made her wonder if I really knew what I was doing. Why should I be afraid of a simple human touch, a frightened person reaching out for some small contact?

Susan could not see herself as I saw her—as a caged, frightened, angry animal, who was making strange noises, who was stiff with fear and constraint, and whose eyes held a rather crazed expression I had never seen before. Rather she saw herself as she truly felt inside—a very frightened little girl who was desperate for some way of connecting to me. Barely able to speak, unable to cry, completely incapable of naming any feeling even if she could speak, she reached out to me in the only way she could.

Unfortunately, she came to the conclusion that I was just like her mother—that I abhorred any physical closeness and was repulsed by her need to touch me. She asked if this was true, but clearly did not accept my answer that it was not. We have discussed this incident many times, and though Susan has attempted to come back from it, she has repeatedly told me that she has not felt really safe with me since this incident.

I should add that not only did Susan conclude early in her treatment that I was not willing to make any physical contact with her, but added that she was a "physical" person—athletic, a good lover, etc.—while characterizing me as verbal, overly-intellectual, nonphysical, and lacking in empathy in many respects. Susan's repeated insults and attempts to degrade my character, disposition, and therapeutic abilities typically followed any disappointment she felt with me. She frequently threatened to terminate, which naturally reminded me of her mother throwing her in the basement or taking her to the orphanage.

From my description I think you can see that treating Susan has not been easy. Even though she is extremely fragile and hurt by the slightest perceived rejection or less-than-ideal response from me, she defends with rigid demands and criticisms. And although she is very hard-working and motivated, her problems in naming any emotion and her inability ever to tell me what she needs or wants, make it very difficult to respond adequately. When I tell her that she did not make herself clear, she responds derisively with, "You know. Or you could've figured it out."

Since our original rupture on the issue of physical contact, Susan has gone in and out of expressing a need for it. During the last 18 months she has taken my hand and held it while she lay on the couch. Like several other patients in the past who have asked for this type of contact, Susan has responded by being more relaxed, expressed that she felt safer, and has been able to tap much deeper levels of emotion at these times. During these periods of contact she has been able to produce what I call "inverted crying." What I mean by this is that she sounds as if she is crying but produces little or no tears.

Occasionally she also has wanted to hug me at the end of a particularly difficult or meaningful session. I, like McLaughlin, believe that non-erotic brief hugs should not be denied to patients who need them because the narcissistic injury caused by refusing causes more harm than ever comes from participating.

I find that most patients who ask for physical contact, and so far they are in the minority, are quite content with having their hands held or receiving a hug. Susan, however, is not. She has repeatedly told me how much she wants and needs for me to hold her. She understands that the point of analysis is for her to understand and accept that she did not get the mothering she needed as a little girl—and to grieve this. Yet she insists that because of her lack of development in experiencing and expressing affect, she can only feel deeply when she is touched.

Her feelings about this relate to another critical incident that occurred between us almost a year ago. Susan had been feeling a tremendous amount of emotion in a particular session and began decompensating when I told her time was up. She sat up on the couch and began shaking and crying, again throwing me this wild-eyed, pleading look. She thrashed slightly back and forth as she sat on the couch, unable to leave. She flashed me a desperate, "Don't just sit there, do something!" look. So I got up from my chair, stepped over to the couch where she was sitting up, sat down next to her, and put my hand on her shoulder. I told her it was okay, that she had lost her boundaries but that she would be all right when she left. She calmed down immediately, but then did something that shocked both of us. She suddenly put her arms around me and placed her head on my breast. I stiffened ever so slightly. But remembering the terrible outcome from the time I had slightly pulled away and was frightened, I did not move. I made the conscious decision to give her a minute to realize what she was doing and to pull away herself. If she did not, then I would have gently put my hands on her arms and moved her away while saying something soothing.

Fortunately, Susan realized what she was doing, felt my lack of participation, and moved away. She thanked me for understanding that she needed something and left. The next day she returned in a mood that can only be described as elation. She proceeded to tell me how much the incident from the day before had meant to her. She told me that when she had her head on my breast she felt a feeling of comfort and love that she has never felt before in her life. She added that she had also become aware of the depth of her own longing to be mothered and to feel loved. And that she realized how little she had ever gotten from her own mother—and how much she hated her for that. She said she couldn't believe the depth and breadth of feeling and insight that resulted from her physical contact with me and thanked me for not pulling away.

What followed was that she said she definitely wanted this to happen again, only next time I would have to be more comfortable with it and participate more instead of merely tolerating the experience. Over the next few days she continued to make references like this, but did not ask me to comment. Finally, about two weeks after this incident, she asked me to tell her how I felt that day. Were her perceptions accurate? Was she right in thinking that I didn't want to hurt her, but that I was slightly uncomfortable with the contact? I said yes. She asked why. I said it was too intimate and potentially sexual—that as much as she perceived herself to be a young child, she was not. She then asked the big question. Does that mean I would not do it again? I said I would not.

Needless to say, she took this news very hard. I watched her bubble bursting as I destroyed any fantasy she had of being emotionally awakened through physical contact with me. I tried, in vain, to explain to her that her wish to be re-mothered by me was perfectly understandable and I was sympathetic to her overwhelming feelings of loss and longing. I reiterated that the objective was for her to feel that pain, and to grieve for what she never got. She repeated that she is too armored to get to that pain—that she needs to be touched in order to feel it. I said I was sorry, but that the best I could do was the limited physical contact we had established.

The past year has been a difficult one for both of us. Out of hurt and anger, she rarely asks for any contact. Yet she is getting better. She has a demanding job now that leaves her less time to dwell on our relation-ship. And she began a relationship with another woman who is very in touch with her feelings and helps my patient to understand herself better. But Susan remains bitter and convinced that she is right and I am wrong. After a break from reading the psychoanalytic literature, she has returned to it with a particular focus in mind. She brings in tales of highly empathic therapists who have touched their patients, including Margaret Little's account of her treatment with Winnicott. She says she identifies with Margaret Little, including her frustration at trying to get adequate treatment. Susan then accuses me of being uptight, unempathic, and so unfailingly arrogant that I dare to think I know better than a great analyst like Winnicott. What can I say?

Discussion

In my prior work on the issue of self-disclosure, I have emphasized that anything the patient repeatedly requests in a heartfelt manner is some-thing he or she probably needs. I have also said that therapists can only say or do what they are honestly comfortable saying or doing. No emotionally dishonest act can be therapeutic. In this regard, I admire Casement's ability to be aware of his own second thoughts and discomfort regarding touching his patient, which lead to his refusal to touch her.

Regarding Susan, her requests for me to hold her, as well as her expressed wish for me to extend her Wednesday night end-of-the-day session, often seem very heartfelt. On the other hand, she admits to me that she conceives of our relationship in physical terms because it is all she knows. She is afraid she will never be able to break down and sob with me because it is something she has never done. When she comes close to these feelings she starts to decompensate, and panics. My holding her is her solution to the fear that short-circuits her and keeps her from staying with the pain and getting the much-needed relief of letting go.

But I am not comfortable with this. I used to question myself and wonder if she really *did* need to be held, in spite of the fact that I couldn't do it, but those doubts have abated as I have watched Susan fend off any inclination to give over. Her need for equality, or even a sense of power over me, seems to motivate her request to be held. This is how she avoids any risk of rejection or humiliation.

Contrary to what she believes, I am not repulsed by the thought of physical contact with her. Rather I feel slightly disturbed at the thought of engaging in a physically intimate act with a patient. Also, I do not share her view that she is really a small child seeking desperately-needed support.

My own feeling about malignant regression is that it is created through the therapist's sharing the patient's unrealities—including any delusion about their actual age. My patient may *feel* like a helpless child, but she is, in fact, a very strong-willed, competent adult who is very sexual. While I very much believe that Susan is sincere, I think she is misguided. On one hand, her claims that she does not want to have sex with me are valid, since there is a part of her that realizes her last treatment was a disaster and that she needs this treatment to work. On the other hand, she frequently fantasizes about living with me, spending the rest of her life with me, and being my lover. It is one thing for her to compartmentalize and split off these conflicting wishes, it is quite another for me to do so.

At the same time, I do understand that Susan needs physical contact at times to help ground her and help her relax enough to feel deeply. So I will continue to provide moving my chair close to the couch, occasional hand-holding, and occasional hugs, because no ill-effects have come from this and because I am comfortable in the giving of it. I feel confident that I have met the standards for therapeutic touch outlined earlier.

The touch is initiated by her, either through asking, reaching out her hand, spontaneously hugging me, or throwing me a nonverbal "would you hug me?" look when she is unsure of my feelings toward her. We discuss how and when the touching occurs and what it means to her. It is congruent with the very deep therapeutic relationship we have. And I only engage in physical contact with Susan, or anyone else, when I am comfortable doing so. If I am not, then I refuse and try to articulate why I have done so. Like Searles and Casement, I have found the refusal of contact to be as therapeutic as the acceptance of it.

For example, some patients seek physical contact when they are angry and afraid of that feeling. My countertransference response to their anger is to refuse the contact, tell them my perception that they are angry, and say that hand-holding is not congruent with this emotional situation.

Physical contact, like any intervention, can be therapeutic or not. If it is done with consideration for the therapist's feelings and needs, as well as the patient's, it is less likely to lead to unseemly intimacies and abuse of the patient.

Gabbard (1996) notes that many therapists who end up having sex with their patients "have self-destructively surrendered to demands for demonstrations of caring." My refusal with Susan strikes me as falling into this category—that I would only do it out of a need to satisfy her longings and demands—rather than because I believed it was the right thing to do.

I also keep in mind that my training has prepared me to *resist* the notion of physical contact rather than to explore this issue openly. McLaughlin (1995) says,

> The topic of touching has always been complicated by its con-nections with the unsettled liabilities of physical intimacy, sexual and aggressive, between the analytic pair. The specter of this ultimate excess has made almost impossible a dispassionate as-sessment of the technical implications of lesser forms of physical contact [pp. 433–434].

He passionately encourages analysts to consider that we have overlooked the prudent use of limited physical contact for therapeutic purposes.

From my own experience I can safely say that I have never had a bad outcome from simple finger- or hand-holding, nor from occasional hug-ging, provided it met the criteria I outlined earlier. I have also noticed that female patients tend to be more physical with me, I think in part because social hugging as a greeting between women has become so common. Men, on the other hand, are more likely to shake my hand on a regular basis as they enter or leave their sessions. My male patients tend to hug me, if at all, only at the end of very emotionally moving sessions.

As to actual holding or rocking and stroking a patient, as Winnicott did with Little, I have never done this, and have difficulty imagining a situation with an adult patient where I would be comfortable doing so. For example, exactly at what point would I say, "I'm sorry, but your time is up for today"? I just can't see this degree of intimacy ever being consistent with maintaining a limited, professional relationship. And the potential for doing harm is great. Once certain boundaries have been crossed, there is no going back. And intimate physical contact could easily become this Rubicon, leaving nothing to move toward responsibly except termination.

In summary, the reports of other clinicians, combined with my own years of experience utilizing limited, nonsexual touching, have convinced me that it can be very appropriate and therapeutic. The fact that it can also be used defensively does not warrant excluding touch as a valid intervention, since all interventions can be used defensively. Limited use of physical contact appears to offer significant benefits to many patients whose experience is beyond words, or who simply need to make the most basic human connection between themselves and their therapists.

Chapter 8

Reflections on the Analyst's Legitimate Power and the Existence of Reality

The fall of the analyst as the ultimate authority has been a welcome one for most analytic clinicians. Secretly knowing that we were often completely in the dark about what was happening, not only with our patients, but also within ourselves, we have been released from clinging to a level of knowledge and authority that was unattainable. On the other hand, many of us are uncomfortable with the philosophy that we cannot be sure of anything, that our opinions and judgments are so subjective that everything we say and think should be questioned and scrutinized. Those who claim to know are called *positivists*, which by the sound of it, would appear to be a good thing. But it is not. For example, this statement from Hoffman (1992), as he delineates his social-constructivist view, demonstrates his clearly *negative* view of positivists.

> What I mean by the positivist or objectivist paradigm is a view of the process in which analysts or psychoanalytic therapists are thought to be capable of standing outside the interaction with the patient so that they can generate rather confident hypotheses and judgements about the patient's history, dynamics, and transference and about what they themselves should do from moment to moment [p. 289].

In an earlier work (1991) Hoffman declared his alternative to the positivist or objectivist view:

> what the analyst seems to understand about his or her own experience and behavior as well as the patient's is always suspect, always susceptible to the vicissitudes of the analyst's own resistance, and always prone to being superseded by another point of view that may emerge [p. 77].

Although I think that Hoffman has made a very significant contribution to the evolution of analytic thought in the area of the relationship between therapist and patient, I do not fully agree with his point of view. It seems to be too much of a pendulum swing in the opposite direction of the analyst being all-knowing. His willingness to question himself is admirable, and I applaud his more egalitarian and mutual philosophy, but does even Hoffman himself question his every thought when he is working with a patient? What is philosophically interesting and high-minded may not be what is clinically useful, or even doable. Keeping an open mind, and seeing the patient as a human being who is capable of enlightening the therapist in all manner of things, and as someone who should have his feelings and thoughts respected, is not the same as believing that everything is relative, or that nothing is knowable. Benjamin (1991), in her discussion of Hoffman's paper on the social-constructivist view, says,

> Once we accept that the analytic situation is one in which we mutually constitute each other, we see that our participation not only skews our understanding but also is the prerequisite for a shared reality. I think that the aspect of shared reality is neglected in Hoffman's model. Living with the incompleteness of self-knowledge and knowledge of the other—the perspectivist dilemma—does not mean that direct recognition of the other's experience through identification is impossible or only skewed [p. 528].

Stern (1992) has also noted that just because both analyst and patient contribute to a construction of the truth does not mean that there is not a separate reality that exists.

Hoffman (1983) was one of the earliest advocates of mutuality in the analytic relationship. In his now classic paper he noted that the patient was, indeed, a credible interpreter of the analyst's experience. In other words, the patient is implicitly seen as someone who could know something about the analyst that the analyst was unaware of in the moment. And I have no qualms about this. Having given the patient his due as a credible interpreter of the analyst's experience, can we accord *less* to the analyst? How can we see ourselves as incapable of that which we have conferred on the patient? Or, as Kernberg (1996) said on this topic,

> If the patient were *not* to assume that the analyst has some legitimate authority and that in entering psychoanalysis, the patient has to accept the leadership authority of an analyst trained to carry out such a treatment, the psychoanalytic relationship would become absurd [p. 143].

It seems to me that our only viable position is the one where both analyst and patient are seen as mutually capable of great accuracy, great error, and everything in between. And this is where the notion of negotiation comes in, each party going back and forth with his or her views and feelings until, as Benjamin says, some shared reality is established. As mutual as this process is, someone must nonetheless be in charge. Granted, this may not always work out. The analyst and patient may speak different languages to the point where hammering out a shared reality is often not possible. Or the analyst, having accepted her responsibility as the leader and facilitator of the therapeutic process, may insist on views of the patient, or approaches to the treatment, that are incompatible with the patient's views and needs. If so, then the pair is best off ending the treatment, allowing both patient and therapist to find better matches.

A rather complicated, but interesting, case example illustrates some of what I am saying about the analytic relationship. Continuing in my use of the case of Susan, she was obviously someone who was very much concerned with power and control. So much so, that she often refused to acknowledge my position as the "leader" in the treatment. Although I have always enjoyed treating patients who feel free to challenge anything I say or do, I must admit to feeling quite frustrated and angry at

Susan for challenging so many things I said or did. You may recall from earlier chapters that this patient found something wrong with every major aspect of my person, my office, and the way I conducted the treatment. The office was too cold and too bright. The couch needed back pillows for shorter patients (like Susan). I charged too much. The sessions were too short (50 minutes). I was too withholding. She needed to be held and touched, not analyzed. This last comment often prompted me to ask her why she stayed in analysis if she really was convinced that she needed extensive physical contact. Yet most of the time I was able to live with these criticisms, often deferring to Susan, for example, turning the heat up, getting pillows for the couch so her feet would touch the floor when she was sitting up, letting her turn lights off that seemed too bright for her, providing minimal physical contact.

What I could *not* live with was Susan refusing to accept most of my observations about her and her behavior. Within the first year of treatment Susan regressed to the demanding state described above. However, as I noted in earlier descriptions of her, she initially presented as one of Krystal's "super-adjusted" alexithymics. Unaware and unconcerned about her inability to emote, she prided herself on her "corporate" demeanor—always cool, collected, and in control. Losing control was for weaklings. Remaining so removed from her own needs and feelings, Susan was stunned by the feelings of neediness and dependency that surfaced when she regressed. She also found her insistent demands and rage at me for not granting many of her requests to be ego-dystonic. Increasingly she stated to me, "I only feel this way with you," or "You are the only person who has ever described me as demanding or controlling. I am known for my reasonableness and self-reliance." Susan maintained this view of herself as the innocent, reasonable, healthy and normal person, telling me that the only reason she had so many conflicts with me was because I was withholding and did not know how to treat her. (When she called my home phone on my day off to ask me a question about dealing with her insurance company, I told her that this was a misuse of my home phone number, which was only for emergencies. She reluctantly ended the conversation with me, but the following Monday defended her calling me on my home phone, saying that this was something important to her. I replied by saying that not only was it not an emergency, it was nothing that could not have waited until Monday.

She argued with me and said if she had it to do over again, she would. Trying to avoid any threats, I simply said that was unacceptable to me, that she should call into my answering machine and leave a message if she wanted to talk with me and I would call her back as soon as I could.)

Had I bought into Susan's reality at that time we both would have become hopelessly lost. Even if I resisted her demands, the treatment would have faltered had I lost confidence in my ability and my own reality-testing. I did my best to be fair to Susan, listening to her complaints and admitting when I had been unreasonable, sadistic, or distant. But she clearly was attempting to be more in control of herself by trying to gain control of the treatment, which I could not allow—for her sake as much as mine. Susan had regressed to what Khan (1972) called the state of "resourceless dependence," an intolerable state of helplessness with accompanying annihilation fears. Like the patient Khan describes in his paper, Susan fought ferociously to avert her state of resourceless dependence, which felt like death.

She often described herself as crazed when she was not in her sessions, and regularly threw "tantrums" when her sessions were over, accusing me of trying to harm her, acting as if she would faint when she had to sit up on the couch and stand to leave, and frequently slamming the door on her way out when she finally left. For her, this was a fight to the death. It was either her or me. If I prevailed, she would be left in a state of emotional annihilation, because her early childhood trauma left her believing that if she gave over, or surrendered, to me that I would do my best to destroy her. She simply could not let that happen. I, on the other hand, knew that I could not let her win this power struggle, that somehow I had to help her to see that giving over to her deepest feelings was *not* submission to me and would not result in her demise.

Although this struggle continued over a year or more, several key things happened. First, I convinced her to see my consulting psychiatrist for medication to reduce the symptoms of her transference-psychosis and her insomnia, which helped her to listen better when we were together. Then I told her point-blank that her view of herself was completely crazy. I told her that the person she described was really a persona she had developed over her lifetime to deal with the verbal and physical abuse at the hands of her parents, and then to deal with the corporate world that did not invite emotional responses. I basically said, "Don't you see that

all of the neediness, dependency, longing, and rage that you feel with me
are aspects of yourself that you buried many years ago? I realize that none
of this has surfaced before, but that doesn't mean *I am causing you to feel
this way through some errors or wrongdoing on my part.* You are feeling this
way because you are regressed and because these feelings have always
been there." I also explained to her what alexithymia was and how she
fit into this category, which she found very interesting. And I told her
that if I was going to continue to treat her she had to be willing to
acknowledge that all the money she was paying me was for a professional
service that I did, indeed, know how to provide. I told her that I was
frankly tired of her turning every observation on me and telling me that
everything I felt was idiosyncratic to me and was my problem. For
example, when I told her how frustrated and angry I felt at times because
of her constant criticism she would reply with something like, "Well,
that's your problem. You take things too personally." Even simple empathy would be rebuked because accepting it left her feeling too vulnerable.
If I said "you seem sad today," she might say something like, "Well, sure.
Haven't *you* ever felt sad?"—as if it were an accusation. When I pointed
out that any observation of mine seemed to be received by her as an
accusation, she told me that she didn't like me focusing on her weaknesses all the time.

When Susan said that she wanted me to admit to my weaknesses, too,
I agreed that this was reasonable if some weakness of mine was affecting
her in the present moment, or had an overall effect on the treatment. I
said we were not here to analyze me, just so that things could be equal.

She had to accept the asymmetry of the relationship, like it or not, or
there was not going to be any treatment. Feeling weak and powerless,
which she certainly had been as a child, was something she had to relive
in her treatment. It was not something she could avoid by constantly
working to equalize things between us. Her pursuit of personal power,
rather than focusing on her true emotional experience, would lead
nowhere.

Susan began to let in what I was saying to her, particularly after one
day when I got angry and confronted her with many of the "realities" I
observed about her that she constantly denied. Since I also emphasized
why I thought she needed to hide from herself—just how vulnerable and
frightened she really was—she began to come around. The day after my

confrontation she came in feeling much more relaxed than usual, and subdued. She quietly told me that I was right. Everything she saw about herself was either humiliating or terrifying, or both. She felt like she was dying, and I was the person who was killing her. She finally began to understand that I was doing my absolute best to help her, and that I was not the enemy. She said she also understood that the relationship had to be asymmetrical, but that this was very difficult for her to accept in every way. She wanted to be more powerful at times when she was feeling weak; she hated the feelings of inferiority she felt when we talked about her problems; and she wanted me to love and need her as much as she loved and needed me. She said the boundaries were almost impossible for her to accept, but she would try. When our adversarial relationship ceased, she began to make real progress.

There is no doubt in my mind that Susan needed me to believe in myself and take the strong stand with her that I did. She was a very powerful person, who drew on her every resource, including her knack for taking accurate readings on other people, to gain the upper hand with me. Had I "lost" this fight, I would have failed her as a therapist. She needed me to set limits with her consistently, be able to assert myself and refuse to be verbally abused, and also tell her when I thought she was being crazy. Without my own convictions regarding "reality," and my willingness to take many stands regarding my authority in the relation-ship, this treatment would most certainly have failed.

The question comes to mind, "Didn't I ever doubt myself?" "Didn't I ever wonder if I was wrong and the patient was right?" Certainly. And sometimes I was wrong, either partially, or completely. But I used the emotional aftermath, for both Susan and myself, to guide me through these periods. If after one of my strong stands, Susan appeared more relaxed and more open, and I also felt comfortable with what I had done, then I accepted that it was therapeutic. If Susan remained as crazed, or got worse, after one of my interventions or if I ruminated about what I had said, or was agitated or depressed, then I would know that something hadn't gone right—that I was wrong in either what I had said or the way I had said it. If Susan simply came to her next session unfazed, then all I knew was that she had not taken in what I had said.

Admittedly, most patients do not require this kind of strong stand on the therapist's part on a consistent basis. But many patients do find ways to test us and be reassured that we are in charge, so that it is safe for them to relinquish their defenses and rely on us to provide a safe environment to do so. Many patients who were forced to grow up too soon, often because overburdened parents capitalized on their precociousness, have established a persona of being super-responsible or super-achieving. In order to maintain this persona and defend against the unsatisfied child-hood dependency needs, these patients are often super-controlling in their relationships. But they secretly long for someone else to be in charge and release them from their prison of overresponsibility. Patients like this will try to control the treatment initially, but really want the therapist to take control so that they can relax and give up their defenses. One young woman I treated early in my career would periodically look at me and say, "you're in charge, right?" After I answered with a confident "yes," then she would give over and explore her deepest feelings. Other patients I have actually had to confront, like Susan, and tell them they were trying to be in control when it was the opposite of what they needed to do. Why are they paying me so much money and not letting me do my job? And it has amazed me how often this approach has been therapeutic, the patients expressing great relief that this burden had been lifted from their shoulders.

Can We Distinguish Between Knowledge and Authority?

When I began writing this section of the chapter I had intended to say that we could distinguish between knowledge and authority, even though they frequently overlap. But as I began writing I soon realized that nothing is truly objective and free from potential bias or distortion, including diagnosis and prognosis. Everything that we learned about psycho-dynamics in our training, assuming that the basic information is correct, is still only objective in theory. In practice, I would have to agree with Hoffman that everything is potentially subjective and biased (although Szasz, 1963, made this point much earlier). Yet, as I stated previously, rather than relinquishing all claims to knowledge and authority, I prefer to look at how we decide that we know something and what we do with that knowledge.

Mitchell (1997) criticizes Kernberg for imagining that "*trying* to be neutral actually makes it possible to *be neutral,* to arrive at a perspec-tiveless vantage point" (pp. 216–217, emphasis Mitchell's). He goes on to say that there are many possible ways of knowing what is happening in the patient's mind, and that different meanings are arrived at through "an active process of composing and arranging them" (p. 218). In this way, both analyst and patient may come up with variations of meaning, neither being necessarily "right" or "wrong." He says that some arrangements are better than others, however.

While I am certainly not prepared to argue against correct interpretations of the patient's or the analyst's experience, I just don't think that correctness is ultimately the determining factor in whether or not the interpretation is therapeutic. A reasonable understanding, or as Mitchell would say, arrangement, is rather the first step toward a therapeutic exchange. Although they are less desirable on a regular basis, misunderstandings and incorrect interpretations are also frequently the starting point for an interaction that is ultimately therapeutic.

Therefore, I think it is not a question of right or wrong. Rather it is more a question of what can the patient hear, comprehend, and use at any given point in time. When I was giving Susan interpretations about her need to protect herself, I was correct, yet my interpretations fell on deaf ears until I had broken through to Susan on an emotional level. What I knew at that point was relatively useless in terms of communicating with her. Therapists used to perseverate with correct interpretations, thinking that eventually the patient would have to accept them. Usually the patient became more defensive and angry instead. By definition, anything that cannot be used productively by the patient is meaningless, regardless of its correctness. Brenner (1996) says, "the fact is that neither analyst nor patient can claim unimpeachable accuracy for any given conjecture. In the majority of cases the analyst is in a better position to decide . . ." (p. 30). I think that many people, including myself, would take issue with Brenner's conclusion that when a difference of opinion exists, the analyst is usually right. Even if this were true, Brenner misses the point entirely. So the analyst is right. If the analyst is right, and the patient doesn't agree, then the analyst has achieved nothing more than self-satisfaction.

A good example of the negotiating technique that I recommend throughout this book can be seen in the following case vignette. Rita, a middle-aged, successful businesswoman came to two consecutive sessions noticeably depressed. She said she had spent two days in bed the past week and was still depressed. As the session evolved she focused on her affair with a married man who works at her office. She said she was frustrated and lonely. She needed more than she was getting from him. Her intense dissatisfaction with the relationship was rather new. Previously she stated that an affair fit perfectly with her busy schedule, and her fears of engulfment. Two weeks ago she returned from a trip to California. Now her lover is out of town for the week. Rita concludes her litany of defensive-sounding complaints with the statement that she saw her lover having lunch with another co-worker, noticeably flirting with her. She said she thinks it is time to end the relationship.

In my mind I am thinking that the reason she sounds so defensive and wants to break up with this man is because of their recent physical separations, which may have stimulated a need for him that she is uncomfortable with. Considering that Rita fears her partner might stray, I asked her if she felt like she wanted to "dump" him because she was afraid he would dump her. She said no, that wasn't it. Normally this would be enough for me to desist, since she did not seem defensive when she told me I was wrong. But she continued to talk about him in a defensive manner, which made me question her. I reiterated my feeling that she was afraid of admitting that he was important to her. She, once again, calmly told me I was wrong. She added that, on the contrary, she was relieved that her lover was out of town right now.

Confused and somewhat frustrated, I engaged her on this level. I talked to Rita the way I would talk to a colleague whom I was consulting on the case, which is what I recommend when treating patients. I told her I just didn't get it. Obviously she was depressed enough to take to her bed, yet she dismissed all of my ideas about why she was depressed, such as her lover's absence and her possible fears of losing him. And nothing else she had revealed up to this point seemed significant enough to cause this period of malaise. I told her I just didn't get it. Could she enlighten me?

She immediately lowered her head in shame and looked away from me. Then she confessed that there was something she hadn't told me. When she was on her trip to California, she had a one night stand with a man she met there. She felt guilty and upset about it and didn't want anyone to know—including me. My response was on the order of, "so that's why you've been so depressed and why you're glad he's out of town. You're ashamed of what you did and this way you don't have to face him.

Saying that you think he might potentially cheat on you really comes from your guilt about cheating on him." To these comments she quietly said, "yes." We were then able to discuss openly both of the important issues at hand. First, her brief affair and the guilt and shame she felt about it, and second, her fears of losing my respect and affection if I knew about it. I think this case illustrates how the patient will hold her own when the analyst is wrong, how the analyst has to accept nondefensive responses from the patient, yet also be true to her own beliefs and feelings, and how when both people reasonably discuss the failure to achieve a shared reality, something is likely to surface that helps clarify the situation.

Patients often respond to unwanted truths by getting drowsy, changing the subject if it is something they cannot know, and become defensively angry if it is something they know but cannot yet bear. When the truth is bearable the patient takes it in, usually becoming still, thoughtful and self-interpretive in response to the analyst's intervention.

This is probably a good time for me to emphasize that I do believe in the power of an accurate interpretation. Most of the emphasis in this volume is on affect and affective communication, both because I see this as the most critically important aspect of treatment, and because I feel it has been given short-shrift in comparison to the emphasis over the years on interpretation. But this is not to say that I do not regularly interpret and retain respect for this valuable and basic tool of the analytic trade. A good interpretation should stimulate the needed affect for producing new learning.

For example, in the case of Sarah, a patient who claimed to be madly in love with me and unable to live without me, her treatment predictably got bogged down in the erotized transference. She repeatedly told me how much she suffered over not having me and said she believed that she could finally be happy if only we could be together. Sarah had been very critical of me throughout the treatment and was often enraged with me. She also had a history of troubled relationships that ended with huge arguments. When the dust cleared, Sarah inevitably believed that she was mistreated or abused. She also ended a relationship with a physician who she felt had behaved unethically toward her and whom she had threatened to report to the licensing board.

I reached a point with Sarah during her pleas to be with me, where I began thinking to myself, "No, you wouldn't be happy if I would be with you. You would become disenchanted very quickly, as you do with everyone. And then you would report me to the licensing board and sue me for malpractice. You are frustrated in this relationship because I have not done anything to justify your defensive rages and you have nowhere to go with your familiar relational pattern of being the victim and then having someone outside of yourself to hate. If I slept with you, then you could hate me and feel justified in trying to destroy me." I realize that this is not the most parsimonious interpretation in the world, but it was what I kept thinking. So finally one day I just said it to her. And to my amazement, she immediately relaxed, her face changing first to shame and then to relief. Then she said she thought I was right, that that is exactly what would happen. We talked about her rage and she brought up her envy of me as an additional stimulus, and the impasse was broken. This case illustrates that complex understandings of the patient's experience do not have to be intellectualized, and that, said in personal terms, can have tremendous emotional power.

Dealing with Seemingly Unfair Criticism from Patients

One aspect of the analyst's authority involves accepting, or rejecting, the patient's truths. Do I, as the analyst, simply take in whatever is said about me or do I beg to differ? Does it matter whether it is an emotional issue or a professional one, for example, the patient who says I am a pain in the neck, compared with the patient who says I am not doing right by him as a therapist? Does mutuality mean that I have the same right to disagree with the patient's point of view as he does with mine; should I, for example, admit to the patient when he is right about my failings, and should I then tell him when I think he is wrong?

I think these are extremely difficult decisions to make. Traditionally, we did not tell our patients if we disagreed with them. Nor did we tell them that we felt misunderstood or abused. We felt obligated to endure even the worst treatment at their hands, hoping that someday they would realize what they were doing. If we couldn't take their abuse we would reach an impasse and either the patient would leave, or we would refer the patient elsewhere. Our traditional position was a rather masochistic one that we rationalized as necessary for the patient's sense of safety and trust. We were supposed to be the people who would tolerate anything and never abandon them.

And I find many therapists today who tolerate all manner of abuse and rationalize it as providing the "containing" function that the patient needs. The only thing you teach an abusive patient when you tolerate their sadistic behavior is that you will willingly participate in the sado-masochistic relational pattern they continually replay. Just because you allow the patient to be the hammer and make yourself the nail, instead of the other way around, doesn't really make things that different. Should we not be teaching our patients how to relate in a healthier way, rather than agreeing to take their place as the victim?

I realize that the argument I am making may sound suspiciously like the worst stereotypic blaming of the patient that we are accustomed to seeing in the literature. But the point I am trying to make is that many patients, either occasionally, or consistently, will test the analyst to see if she is able to stand up for herself in a way that the patient has never been able to. If the analyst responds to this test by remaining passive and allowing abuse, then she has failed. If the analyst turns the tables, as we have often seen in the literature, by sadistically barraging the patient with insulting or accusatory interpretations, then she also fails. The only way for the analyst to succeed is by expressing her honest feelings and setting limits that create a respectful, safe environment for both parties.

When I am teaching these ideas to other therapists, I am often asked if I immediately stand up to any patient who dares to use obscenities toward me or insult me. Of course not. Every patient needs to know that he can get angry with his therapist, and spontaneous anger often contains insults or four-letter words. I do think it is essential for the therapist to be understanding when a patient feels pain and anger. The line I am drawing pertains to times when the patient is out of control and has gone far beyond expressing anger or displeasure. If the patient really has a point, which is often the case, but has chosen an inappropriate way to express it, then I tell him so. I might say something like, "I understand you are very angry with me, and that's not a problem, but I will not tolerate repeated personal insults, yelling, or swearing at me. Even though you have a right to be angry, you don't have a right to be abusive. Can you try to find a way to tell me why you're so angry without assaulting me?"

Patients who abuse their therapists usually have a history of verbally abusing others and losing relationships because of this. They are looking

for someone to help them get in control of themselves. This is part of the
affective regulation I talked about earlier. Placating them or abandoning
them is simply a repetition of what always happens in their lives. I am
frankly amazed at the number of times I have heard stories about patients
with the diagnosis of borderline personality disorder who go for treatment
and, instead, receive nothing but empathy. These patients talk about how
bad they feel, how no one does right by them, how everyone else needs
to change, and many therapists simply empathize with these distorted
and narcissistic views of the world. Secretly, the therapist may be thinking, "Boy you're a pain, no wonder no one likes you," yet says nothing.
Often the therapist needs to confront the patient about his treatment of
others, as well as his treatment of the therapist. Again, out of fears of
being judgmental, or of alienating the patient, therapists may abdicate
their responsibility to confront the patient constructively with the consequences of his behavior. Insult is inevitably added to injury, as the
therapist hides her negative feelings and thoughts about the patient,
resulting in an emotional distance that inhibits any real progress.

There are patients who may be verbally abusive toward their analysts
who are otherwise inhibited outside of treatment. Naturally, you would
give these patients more leeway because they are learning how to express
anger for the first time. If they become sadistic it may come as a shock to
them as well as the therapist. But it needs to be addressed, nonetheless.
They still need to find a constructive way to express their anger, even if
it is not a frequent event.

I find that most therapists err in the direction of being too accepting,
or of guiltily feigning acceptance when they are faced with a difficult
patient. The issue gets even more complicated when the patient's criticisms are valid. How far do you let someone go when you know they are
right? As I said, most therapists go too far in indulging the patient's
negative behavior. When I suggest to other therapists that they could be
more assertive, they often balk at this, claiming that they might harm the
patient or inhibit his expressions of anger in the future. I think these are
unrealistic fears. I have never seen any evidence that a patient was
harmed by my standing up to his verbal abuse. In fact, quite the contrary.
These moments are usually very therapeutic. I will admit that the patient
does think twice before being abusive in the future, and may inhibit his
anger at times out of fear of being abusive. But this is easily identifiable

and can be worked through. Often patients will say to me, "I'm really angry with you, but you got mad at me the last time, so now I don't want to tell you." Then I remind them that the reason I was upset was because they were abusive, not because they were angry, and I encourage them to tell me what they are feeling. For patients who only know how to express their anger through verbal abuse, a little inhibition is not the end of the world, and will certainly serve them better outside of the treatment than the explosive outbursts many of them are known for.

Krystal (1988, 1997) says that many therapists are themselves al-exithymic, meaning that they cannot express their own feelings, and therefore cannot use self-disclosure as a therapeutic intervention. I really have no answer for this problem, other than to question their vocational choice. Another obstacle to being emotionally honest and assertive with patients comes from most therapists having been peace-makers in their own families. Often the person who chooses to become a therapist was the sensitive child who shored up a depressed parent, or tried to calm the waters and placate an angry parent. Lacking any real power or control, the child who serves as a budding therapist to her troubled family is not in a position to set limits or be confrontive. So you might say that our earliest "training" as therapists encourages endless empathy, under-standing, and tolerance. These are important therapeutic skills, but so are emotional honesty and the ability to protect yourself and your patient. Personally, I would like to see this undeveloped assertive and expressive side of therapists emphasized in training programs, since it is frequently not part of the communication skills most therapists possess at the outset.

Listening to patients' negative feelings and complaints can be a difficult and trying task. It is inevitable that we be defensive at times, simply because we are human. When a patient notes that I am being defensive and informs me that I should not be because I am a therapist, I reply by saying that ideally I would not be defensive, but in reality I will be at times. Sometimes being able to admit it is the best I will do. I find that I often gain insight into my own motivations after a session is over, when I am no longer on the spot. So I may tell a patient who has asked, that I am not sure why I am being defensive, but I will give it considerable thought and let them know at the next session.

Schwaber (1996) discusses the problems inherent in listening to the patient's criticisms of the analyst, noting how contradictory they may be.

One patient tells me I talk too much; another, that I don't talk enough. I feel my degree of activity with each of them is about equivalent. One patient said she felt at my mercy, that I assumed all the control around schedule and fees; I thought, me? But it's I who's been making every effort to be responsive to her work requirements and her financial needs; I was being so flexible, I believed, while she was not [p. 6].

Schwaber's comments bring up a multitude of issues involved in listening to criticism from patients. First, of course, is the traditional view of the interaction, which states that the patient is being irrational and not seeing Schwaber accurately. This distortion means she has succeeded in stimulating the transference. The patient is *supposed* to see Schwaber as someone other than who she is in reality. And if Schwaber, or any analyst, rushes in to contradict the patient, then the transference will be squashed. And, in most instances, I agree with this view. We want our patients to freely express their feelings, thoughts and expectations, knowing full well that this will probably involve distorted views of themselves, or us, at certain times.

What we have learned over the years is that simply telling patients that they are projecting their feelings toward their mothers onto us was not terribly helpful. Acknowledging what we said or did to stimulate their feelings, even if some distortion is involved, has proved to be more helpful and keeps us in the moment.

Yet another step forward in analytic treatment has yet to be fully accepted and implemented. Once the transference has been fully developed, the patient often solicits honest reactions from the analyst. For example, Schwaber notes her confusion when different patients want different things from her. I was surprised by this comment, because it seems self-evident that one patient may need for the analyst to be reserved and quiet, while another needs a high level of activity. It is part of our job to adjust our level of activity in accordance with our patients' needs. But what about her reference to the patient who thinks she's so controlling when Schwaber feels she has gone out of her way to be flexible? Should she tell her how she feels, or should she be silent, noting that the patient may well have felt unappreciated and unfairly assessed as Schwaber may now feel at her hands?

On these issues I think that timing is everything. Initially, when a patient makes any observation about us, positive or negative, we are inclined to greet it with a mixture of interest and curiosity. Why does the patient feel this way, or think this way, and how does it fit with everything else we know about him? If the analyst feels the observation is correct, the patient's repetitions of it may have little effect. But if the analyst strongly feels that the patient is wrong, for example, that he has overidealized the analyst or has unfairly criticized her, feelings of discomfort and even alienation, begin to build. As time passes, and more repetitions occur, the analyst may cringe, or become angry, or withdraw from the interaction. Once the analyst can no longer unequivocally accept what the patient is saying, what does she do?

I think she should tell the truth about what she is feeling. In Schwaber's example of the patient who insists on labeling her as controlling, when she bends over backwards for her, I think she should tell her she is wrong. Using the example of Susan yet again, I had a similar situation with her. In spite of my doing everything I could to give her the session times she needed, and altering the lighting, temperature, and other things in the room, and reducing the fee for her, she insisted on her view that I was overcontrolling and that everything had to be done my way. In the beginning these criticisms just bounced off me. I saw them as projections of her own need for control and her parents' control of her. After hearing this a few more times, it started to irritate me slightly, but was still something I could accept. Months later, after many very difficult and stressful sessions where I felt I turned myself inside out to try and work with her, Susan repeated these accusations. Now I was getting really angry. Finally I just said to her, "This is ridiculous. How can you possibly say this to me in light of all of the ways I have accommodated you?" She laughed out loud and said that was a joke. *She was the one who did all the accommodating, not me.* I then listed all the things I have mentioned previously and told her I was exasperated, angry, and just plain sick of hearing all these absurdly untrue things.

Susan was surprised at my strong feelings, but then felt free to have her own strong feelings. She told me how frustrated she was with the asymmetry of the relationship, and that she really had not thought at all about what I had done to accommodate her. She said she was stunned by how long the list was, and understood now why I looked angry when she said I did nothing for her. She went on to say that she felt controlled in spite of my flexibility, because she still wanted so many things that she couldn't have, like more time with me, the power to extend the sessions if she wanted to, and most of all, to be as important to me as I was to her. This encounter was far more therapeutic and freeing for both of us than if I had simply remained silent, or asked Susan if she was trying to make me feel angry or unappreciated as she had in her life, which is really a backhanded self-disclosure posing as an interpretation (see Cooper, 1997).

Not that this encounter ended Susan's unfair criticisms of me. It didn't. But she did stop her wholesale negating of everything I had done, which helped me to feel less alienated from her and more able to be present when she did criticize me. Talking things out also helped me to see how difficult the treatment situation was for Susan, how it took everything she had to conform to the basic ground rules, none of which she entirely approved of, many of which she honestly felt were inherently unfair and unreasonable (like the fee structure and time limits).

Susan is so caught up in how she has been mistreated in life that it never occurs to her that she might be mistreating others. Only a strong stand by the analyst can provide that valuable feedback. Hirsch and Roth (1995) note Sullivan's early contribution in this regard:

> The role of the analyst is to know the patient as others do and to facilitate awareness of how the patient is viewed by others. The analyst is a consensual validator who makes the patient aware of who he or she *really is.* ... Sullivan believed that the analyst's stance, optimally, leads to a breakdown in rigid patterns of living that the patient has perpetuated [p. 268].

Sullivan understood that we all develop personas as a natural defense against aspects of ourselves that are not fully accepted by our caretakers or society. The more defended, the greater the persona. And it is the analyst's role to help the patient break down that persona so that more authentic feelings and thoughts can surface and be integrated with each other instead of being compartmentalized or split off. It is part of the analyst's authority to refuse to accept anything in the patient that seems false. Empathy alone is often not enough to break through the rigid patterns of thinking, feeling, and behaving that so many patients have developed. I hasten to add that sometimes the patient will perform the same service for the analyst, particularly with regard to the analyst's need to see herself as the perpetually good person or good mother.

An important aspect of the analyst's authority involves giving the patient this valuable feedback and not backing down from her own internal experiencing in response to the patient. In this respect, we may say that both analyst and patient must have the last word on their own experience, with each person having the option to use or discard what the other reveals to them.

Failures in Authority

I find it interesting that we infrequently note the many failures in authority that occur on a daily basis. For example, I have heard many therapists say that certain patients are constantly delinquent in their payments, yet the therapist does little or nothing about it. Often the analyst may interpret why the patient is not paying and simply wait to see if this has the desired effect. From my experience, any patient who is consistently late in paying his bill has these problems with other bills and obligations as well. And I have never found that interpreting the patient's passive-aggressive behavior has much impact, even when the patient honestly sees what he is doing. I have always had to insist on payment from these patients, and do. And my insistence on being paid in a timely manner, usually results in the patient paying other bills promptly as well. If the patient has some financial hardship I will make the appropriate arrangement, but always emphasize that this is something we need to discuss, not something to be ignored in hopes that it will go away.

The literature is also replete with examples of acting-out by patients while the analyst remains passive. I previously (Maroda, 1991) cited the example of Silverman reporting a case where the patient went from being relatively poor to rich, and Silverman did not raise the fee. Rather he waited for the patient to offer to raise the fee, which is an abdication of the analyst's power and authority. The very same patient tried to provoke Silverman by getting mud on his new couch. Again, no personal response. Even famous analysts like Winnicott were often masochistically passive when their patients acted out against them. Little (1990), in her account of her treatment with Winnicott, noted that she deliberately smashed a vase in his office that appeared to mean something to him. She praised

him for saying nothing. When she came to her next session she found
that he had replaced the broken vase with an exact duplicate. Little was
not told to clean up the mess she had made, or asked to pay for the vase.
Does this seem like a normal human response, let alone a therapeutic
one? We cannot know why Winnicott did not express his feelings about
Little's behavior, but his failure to hold her accountable in any way strikes
me as complete absence of authority.

Other failures in authority include doing nothing when a patient
repeatedly engages in self-destructive behaviors, or in behaviors that
harm others; refusing to confront a patient who intrudes on the analyst's
privacy, such as, inappropriate use of the analyst's home phone, stalking
the analyst, using extraneous sources to discover personal or financial
information about the analyst, etc.; and not adequately preparing patients for the length of time and the amount of emotional pain that the
treatment will require.

Again, I have seen therapists who do no more than question a patient
who is violating their privacy to the extreme, who will not say no to
unreasonable requests by patients, like phone calls or postcards when the
analyst is on vacation (although this is complicated by many analysts'
need to be needed); who do not stand up to verbally abusive patients;
and who placate patients simply to keep the peace. Even though we all
do these things at some time or another, I think it is important to locate
these behaviors within the realm of failures in authority, just as it is
important to locate constructive behaviors within the realm of what is
therapeutic.

The old stereotypic analyst remained passive and unmoved by anything the patient did. She may have honestly been filled with emotion.
She may have desperately wanted to confront the patient, but felt she
could not. Or she may have been content to remain removed from the
action, feeling complacent or secretly superior to the obviously distressed
patient. Remnants of this stereotype remain with us in a marked tendency
for analysts to avoid active involvement with their patients and overvalue
passivity and withdrawal. Ultimately, the analyst's real authority and
power come from her continued emotional presence and ability to not
only maintain the proper boundaries of the professional relationship, but
also to promote the emotional honesty and integrity of her patients and
herself.

Conclusion

A s always, I find that the ambitions I brought to this book when I began writing it have not been realized, in that I find it impossible to do justice to the complexity of analytic work, particularly the intricacies of the relationship. What I can imagine in my mind always falls short of what I am able to articulate in a linear fashion. And perhaps this cognitive limitation is part of what makes analytic treatment so difficult. Just as when we write, we ultimately must make do with what we can verbalize, knowing it will never live up to our actual experience. What we know and feel at multiple levels can never be adequately named. Yet through the process of attempting to name what we feel and organize what we think, we learn more. As Flannery O'Connor reputedly said, "I write to discover what I know."

So we struggle to find the best words we can, both to communicate with our patients in the treatment setting, and to talk with each other about what we do. Yet what we struggle to describe, to *name*, is always something that has first been felt. If nothing else, I hope I have adequately made the point that felt emotion, on the part of both the patient and the therapist, is the key to the therapeutic enterprise.

Virtually every chapter in this book places heavy emphasis on affect; affect known and affect unknown; affect expressed and affect denounced or disavowed; affect received and affect deflected or deferred; emotional honesty and emotional dishonesty. I have pressed for a more humbling view of both ourselves and the process, not in the interests of devaluing the world of analysis, but rather in the interest of making it more human and more realistic.

Although I speak at length about our weaknesses and our flaws, as well as those of our patients, I still believe in what we do. I have argued for the analyst's greater personal involvement, including affective self-disclosure, because I believe that the key to our success lies in our emotional availability and emotional honesty, not in our ability to remain above the fray. A psychoanalyst friend of mine said that he never regretted going to medical school, in spite of the fact that his medical knowledge was of limited use in psychoanalysis. He said that he will never forget helping in a delivery when he was only a medical student. There was something about that primal experience, he said, that he would never forget and would reflect on for years to come. He recalled being told to reach in and gently pull the baby out as the mother pushed—and how exhilarated and amazed he was to see this bloody living thing coming out of a woman's body, squiggling and looking angry at having been taken so precipitously from the womb. He looked down at his arms, covered in blood to the elbow, and was filled with primitive wonder and fear. He told me that this turned out be a perfect metaphor for what was required of him as an analyst.

Spezzano (1993) reflected on the patient's wish for emotional engagement with the analyst in a way that seems appropriate to this conversation.

> Each analysand wants the frustrating and painful components of his emotional fingerprint or emblem to be transformed by the analyst, wants the analyst to have the power that the transformational object once had, and wants his affective core to be open again to direct and immediate transformation by the other. As one analysand put it, "I most value something if it immediately changes the way I feel" [p. 226].

And I agree with Spezzano's patient. I, too, value most what changes the way I feel. I say this with the confidence that anything that changes the way I feel will also change the way I think. When I lecture to therapists,

I routinely ask them what they remember most about their personal analysis or psychotherapy. Inevitably, it is some moment of shared emotion, or tender feelings toward the therapist in an instant of vulnerability. Spezzano's patient is not alone. The research on emotion and cognition, described in this book, confirms the view that we cognitively process events in a different and more meaningful way when we feel deeply. This is how literature changes us, this is how religion changes us, this is how theater and music change us, this is how therapy changes us.

The spirit of this book lies in the imperfect pursuit of emotional truth, the fact that we will inevitably achieve something only if we are willing to roll up our sleeves and immerse ourselves in our own primitive emotions and those of our patients. I have learned from my own experience that I only really help patients who move me, who force me to feel things I'd often rather not, and who force me to know things about myself that I don't always like. And I try to do the same for them.

References

Aron, L. (1991), The patient's experience of the analyst's subjectivity. *Psychoanal. Quart.*, 1:29–51.

⸻ (1992), Interpretation as expression of the analyst's subjectivity. *Psychoanal. Dial.*, 2:475–507.

⸻ (1996), *A Meeting of Minds*. Hillsdale: NJ: The Analytic Press.

Averill, J. (1994), Emotions unbecoming and becoming. In: *The Nature of Emotion: Fundamental Questions*, ed. P. Eckman & R. Davidson. New York: Oxford University Press, pp. 265–269.

Balint, M. (1968), *The Basic Fault*. London: Tavistock.

Basch, M. (1991), The significance of a theory of affect. *J. Amer. Psychoanal. Assn.*, 39(Sup.):291–304.

Benedek, T. (1953), Dynamics of the countertransference. *Bull. Menn. Clin.*, 17:201–208.

Benjamin, J. (1991), Commentary on Irwin Z. Hoffman's discussion: Toward a social constructivist view of the psychoanalytic situation. *Psychoanal. Dial.*, 1:525–533.

Bion, W. R. (1959), Attacks on linking. *Internat. J. Psycho-Anal.*, 40:308–315.

Blum, H. (1991), Affect theory and the theory of technique. *J. Amer. Psychoanal. Assn.*, 39(Sup.):265–289.

Boesky, D. (1982), Acting out: A reconsideration of the concept. *Internat. J. Psycho-Anal.*, 63:39–55.

Bollas, C. (1986), The transformational object. In: *The British School of Psychoanalysis: The Independent Tradition*, ed. G. Kohon. London: Free Association Books, pp. 83–100.

—————— (1987), *The Shadow of the Object: Psychoanalysis of Unthought Known*. New York: Columbia University Press.

Bower, G. (1994), Some relations between emotions and memory. In: *The Nature of Emotion: Fundamental Questions*, ed. P. Eckman & R. Davison. New York: Oxford University Press, pp. 303–305.

Brenner, C. (1996), The nature of knowledge and the limits of authority in psychoanalysis. *Psychoanal. Quart.*, 65:21–31.

Brody, L. (1993), On understanding gender differences in the expression of emotion. In: *Human Feelings: Explorations in Affect Development and Meaning*, ed. S. Ablon, D. Brown, E. Khantzian & J. Mack. Hillsdale, NJ: The Analytic Press, pp. 87–121.

—————— & Harrison, R. (1987), Developmental changes in children's abilities to match and label emotionally laden situations. *Motiv. & Emotion*, 2:347–365.

Brown, D. (1993), Affective development, psychopathology, and adaptation. In: *Human Feelings: Explorations in Affect Development and Meaning*, ed. S. Ablon, D. Brown, E. Khantzian & J. Mack. Hillsdale, NJ: The Analytic Press, pp. 5–66.

Casement, P. (1982), Some pressures on the analyst for physical contact during the re-living of an early trauma. *Internat. Rev. of Psycho-Anal.*, 9:279–286.

—————— (1985), *On Learning from the Patient*. London: Tavistock.

Chused, J. (1991), The evocative power of enactments. *J. Amer. Psychoanal. Assn.*, 39:615–640.

—————— (1996), The therapeutic action of psychoanalysis: Abstinence and informative experiences. *J. Amer. Psychoanal. Assn.*, 44:1047–1071.

—————— (1997), Discussion of "Observing–participation, mutual enactment, and the new classical models," by Irwin Hirsch, Ph.D. *Contemp. Psychoanal.*, 33:263–277.

Clore, G. (1994), Why emotions are felt. In: *The Nature of Emotion: Fundamental Questions*, ed. P. Eckman & R. Davison. New York: Oxford University Press, pp. 103–111.

Clyman, R. (1991), The procedural organization of emotions. *J. Amer. Psychoanal. Assn.*, 39(Sup.):349–382.

Compton, A. (1975), Aspects of psychoanalytic intervention. In: *Alterations in Defenses During Psychoanalysis: Aspects of Psychoanalytic Intervention*, ed. B. Fine & H. Waldhorn. New York: International Universities Press, pp. 23–97.

Cooper, S. (1997), The countertransference surface in analyst disclosure and virtual disclosure. Presented at American Psychological Assn. (Div. 39) meetings, Denver, CO, February.

Deleuze, D. (1977), Intellectuals and power: A conversation between Michel Foucault and Gilles Deleuze. In: *Language, Counter-memory, Practice: Selected Essays and Interviews by Michel Foucault*, ed. D. Bouchard (trans. D. Bouchard & S. Simon). Ithaca, NY: Cornell University Press, pp. 205–217.

Ehrenberg, D. (1992), *The Intimate Edge*. New York: Norton.

———— (1995), Self-disclosure and analytic space. *Contemp. Psychoanal.*, 31:213–228.

Epstein, L. (1995), Self-disclosure and analytic space. *Contemp. Psychoanal.*, 31:229–236.

Fast, I. (1992), The embodied mind: Toward a relational perspective. *Psychoanal. Dial.*, 2:389–409.

Ferenczi, S. (1932), *The Clinical Diary of Sándor Ferenczi*, ed. J. Dupont (trans. M. Balint & N. Z. Jackson). Cambridge, MA: Harvard University Press, 1988.

Finnell, J. (1985), Narcissistic problems in analysts. *Internat. J. Psycho-Anal.*, 66:433–445.

———— (1986), The merits and problems with the concept of projective identification. *Psychoanal. Rev.*, 73:103–120.

Forrester, J. (1990), *The Seductions of Psychoanalysis*. Cambridge, UK: Cambridge University Press.

Friedman, L. (1997), Ferrum, ignis, and medicina: Return to the crucible. *J. Amer. Psychoanal. Assn.*, 45:22–36.

Gabbard, G. (1995), Countertransference: The emerging common ground. *Internat. J. Psycho-Anal.*, 76:475–485.

———— (1996), Lessons to be learned from the study of sexual boundary violations. *Amer. J. Psychother.*, 50:311–322.

Gehrie, M. (1996), On the foundations of cure in psychoanalysis. *Psychoanal. Inq.*, 16:184–201.

Gerson, S. (1996), Neutrality, resistance, and self-disclosure in an intersubjective psychoanalysis. *Psychoanal. Dial.*, 6:623–645.

Ghent, E. (1990), Masochism, submission, surrender. *Contemp. Psychoanal.*, 26:108–136.

Gill, M. (1982), *Analysis of Transference, Vol. I.* New York: International Universities Press.

Goldberg, A. (1992), A shared view of the world. In: *The Common Ground of Psychoanalysis*, ed. R. Wallerstein. Northvale, NJ: Aronson, pp. 109–119.

Goodman, M. & Teicher, A. (1988), To touch or not to touch. *Psychother.*, 25:492–500.

Gorkin, M. (1987), *The Uses of Countertransference*. Northvale, NJ: Aronson.

Greenberg, J. (1995), Self-disclosure: Is it psychoanalytic? *Contemp. Psychoanal.*, 31:193–205.

Greenson, R. (1967), *The Technique and Practice of Psychoanalysis*. New York: International Universities Press.

———— (1971), The "real" relationship between the patient and the psychoanalyst. In: *The Unconscious Today*, ed. M. Kanzer. New York: International Universities Press, pp. 213–232.

Grinberg, L. (1979), Countertransference and projective identification. In: *Countertransference: The Therapist's Contribution to the Therapeutic Situation*, ed. L. Epstein & A. Feiner. Northvale, NJ: Aronson, pp. 161–191.

Grotstein, J. (1981), *Splitting and Projective Identification*. Northvale, NJ: Aronson.

———— (1994), Projective identification reappraised. Part 1. *Contemp. Psychoanal.*, 30:708–746.

———— (1995), Projective identification reappraised. Part 2. *Contemp. Psychoanal.*, 31:479–511.

———— (1997), "Mens sane in corpore sano": The mind and body as an "odd couple" and as an oddly coupled unity. *Psychoanal. Inq.*, 17:204–222.

Heimann, P. (1950), On countertransference. *Internat. J. Psycho-Anal.*, 31:81–84.

Hidas, A. (1981), Psychotherapy and surrender: A psychospiritual perspective. *J. Transpersonal Psych.*, 13:27–32.

Hirsch, I. (1993), Countertransference enactments and some issues related to external factors in the analyst's life. *Psychoanal. Dial.*, 3:343–366.

———— (1994), Countertransference love and theoretical model. *Psychoanal. Dial.*, 4:171–192.

———— (1995), Changing conceptions of unconscious. *Contemp. Psychoanal.*, 31:263–276.

Hoffman, I. (1983), The patient as interpreter of the analyst's experience. *Contemp. Psychoanal.*, 19:389–422.

———— (1991), Discussion: Toward a social-constructivist view of the psychoanalytic situation. *Psychoanal. Dial.*, 2:567–570.

———— (1992), Some practical implications of a social-constructivist view of the psychoanalytic situation. *Psychoanal. Dial.*, 2:287–304.

———— (1994), Dialectical thinking and therapeutic action in the psychoanalytic process. *Psychoanal. Quart.*, 63:187–218.

Jacobs, T. (1986), On countertransference enactments. *J. Amer. Psychoanal. Assn.*, 34:289–307.

———— (1995), Discussion of Jay Greenberg's paper. *Contemp. Psychoanal.*, 31:237–245.

Josephs, L. (1995), Countertransference as an expression of the analyst's narrative strategies. *Contemp. Psychoanal.*, 31:345–379.

Kelly, V. (1996), Affect and the redefinition of intimacy. In: *Knowing Feeling: Affect, Script and Psychotherapy*, ed. D. Nathanson. New York: Norton, pp. 55–104.

Kernberg, O. (1987), Projection and projective identification: Developmental and clinical aspects. *J. Amer. Pschoanal. Assn.*, 35:795–819.

———— (1996), The analyst's authority in the psychoanalytic situation. *Psychoanal. Quart.*, 65:137–157.

Khan, M. (1972), Dread of surrender to resourceless dependence in the analytic situation. *Internat. J. Psycho-Anal.*, 53:225–230.

Klein, M. (1946), Notes on some schizoid mechanisms. In: *Envy and Gratitude and Other Works—1943–1966*. New York: Delacorte, pp. 1–24.

Kohut, H. (1971), *Analysis of the Self*. New York: International Universities Press.

———— (1977), *The Restoration of the Self*. New York: International Universities Press.

———— (1984), *How Does Analysis Cure?* ed. A. Goldberg & P. Stepansky. Chicago: University of Chicago Press.

Kraut, R. & Johnston, R. (1979), Social and emotional messages of smiling: An ethological approach. *J. Personality & Soc. Psych.*, 37:1539–1553.

Krystal, H. (1988), *Integration and Self-Healing: Affect, Trauma, Alexithymia*. Hillsdale, NJ: The Analytic Press.

———— (1997), Desomatization and the consequences of infantile psychic trauma. *Psychoanal. Inq.*, 17:126–150.

Laplanche, J. & Pontalis, J. (1973), *The Language of Psycho-Analysis*, trans. D. Nicholson-Smith. London: Hogarth Press.

Langs, R. (1978), *The Listening Process*. Northvale, NJ: Aronson.

LeDoux, J. (1994), Memory versus emotional memory in the brain. In: *The Nature of Emotion: Fundamental Questions*, ed. P. Eckman & R. Davidson. New York: Oxford University Press, pp. 311–312.

Levenson, E. (1990), Reply to Hoffman. *Contemp. Psychoanal.*, 26:299–304.

———— (1994), Beyond countertransference: Aspects of the analyst's desire. *Contemp. Psychoanal.*, 30:691–707.

———— (1996), Aspects of self-revelation and self-disclosure. *Contemp. Psychoanal.*, 32:237–248.

Little, M. (1951), Countertransference and the patient's response to it. *Internat. J. Psycho-Anal.*, 32:32–40.

———— (1957), "R"—The analyst's total response to his patient's needs. *Internat. J. Psycho-Anal.*, 38:240–254.

_____ (1990), *Psychotic Anxieties and Containment*. Northvale, NJ: Aronson.

Loewald, H. W. (1960), On the therapeutic action of psycho-analysis. *Internat. J. Psycho-Anal.*, 41:16–33.

Lomas, P. (1987), *The Limits of Interpretation*. New York: Penguin.

Malin, A. & Grotstein, J. (1966), Projective identification in the therapeutic process. *Internat. J. Psycho-Anal.*, 56:163–177.

Maroda, K. (1991), *The Power of Countertransference*. Chichester, UK: Wiley.

_____ (1995a), Show some emotion: Completing the cycle of affection communication. Presented at Division of Psychoanalysis (39) meeting, American Psychological Assn., Santa Monica, CA.

_____ (1995b), Projective identification and countertransference interventions: Since feeling is first. *Psychoanal. Rev.*, 82:229–247.

_____ (1998), Why mutual analysis failed: The case of Ferenczi and RN. *Contemp. Psychoanal.*, 34:115–132.

Masson, J. (1984), *The Assault on Truth: Freud's Suppression of the Seduction Theory*. New York: Farrar Straus & Giroux.

McDougall, J. (1978), *Plea for a Measure of Abnormality*. New York: International Universities Press.

_____ (1982), Alexithymia: A psychoanalytic viewpoint. *Psychother. and Psychosom.*, 38:81–90.

_____ (1989), *Theaters of the Body: A Psychoanalytic Approach to Psychosomatic Illness*. New York: Norton.

McLaughlin, J. (1991), Clinical and theoretical aspects of enactment. *J. Amer. Psychoanal. Assn.*, 39:595–614.

_____ (1995), Touching limits in the analytic dyad. *Psychoanal. Quart.*, 64:433–465.

_____ (1996), Power, authority and influence in the analytic dyad. *Psychoanal. Quart.*, 65:201–235.

Meissner, W. (1989), The therapeutic action of psychoanalysis: Strachey revisited. *Psychoanal. Inq.*, 9:140–159.

Miller, A. (1981), *Prisoners of Childhood: The Drama of the Gifted Child*. New York: Basic Books.

Mitchell, S. (1988), *Relational Concepts in Psychoanalysis*. Cambridge, MA: Harvard University Press.

_____ (1997), *Influence and Autonomy in Psychoanalysis*. Hillsdale, NJ: The Analytic Press.

Modell, A. (1994), Common ground or divided ground? *Psychoanal. Quart.*, 14:201–211.

Nathanson, D. (1996), Some closing thoughts on affect, scripts, and psychotherapy. In: *Knowing Feeling: Affect, Script and Psychotherapy*, ed. D. Nathanson. New York: Norton, pp. 379–408.

Ogden, T. (1982), *Projective Identification and Psychotherapeutic Technique*. Northvale, NJ: Aronson.

Orange, D. (1995), *Emotional Understanding*. New York: Guilford.

Panel (1992), Enactments in psychoanalysis, reported by M. Johan. *J. Amer. Psychoanal. Assn.*, 40:827–841.

Panskepp, J. (1994), Subjectivity may have evolved in the brain as a simple value-coding process that promotes the learning of new behaviors. In: *The Nature of Emotion: Fundamental Questions*, ed. P. Eckman & R. Davidson. New York: Oxford University Press, pp. 313–315.

Parkinson, B. (1996), Emotions are social. *Brit. J. Psych.*, 87:663–683.

Racker, H. (1968), *Transference and Countertransference*. New York: International Universities Press.

Reich, A. (1950), Further remarks on countertransference. *Internat. J. Psycho-Anal.*, 32:25–31.

Renik, O. (1993), Analytic interaction: Conceptualizing technique in light of the analyst's irreducible subjectivity. *Psychoanal. Quart.*, 62:553–571.

_____ (1995), The ideal of the anonymous analyst and the problem of self-disclosure. *Psychoanal. Quart.*, 64:466–495.

Richards, A., Bachant, J. & Lynch, A. (1997), Interaction in the transference/countertransference continuum. Presented at International Psychoanalytic Association meetings, Barcelona, Spain, July 25.

Sandler, J. (1976), Countertransference and role-responsiveness. *Internat. Rev. Psycho-Anal.*, 3:43–47.

Schafer, R. (1970), The psychoanalytic vision of reality. *Internat. J. Psycho-Anal.*, 51:279–297.

_____ (1976), *A New Language for Psychoanalysis*. New Haven, CT: Yale University Press.

Scharff, J. (1992), *Projective and Introjective Identification and the Use of the Therapist's Self*. Northvale, NJ: Aronson.

Schlessinger, N. & Robbins, F. (1975), The psychoanalytic process: Recurrent patterns of conflict and changes in ego functions. *J. Amer. Psychoanal. Assn.*, 23:761–782.

_____ & _____ (1983), *A Developmental View of the Psychoanalytic Process: Follow-up Studies and Their Consequences*. New York: International Universities Press.

Schore, A. (1994), *Affect Regulation and the Origin of the Self: The Neurobiology of Emotional Development*. Hillsdale, NJ: Lawrence Erlbaum Associates.

Schwaber, E. (1996), Toward a definition of the term and concept of interaction: Its reflection in analytic listening. *Psychoanal. Inq.*, 16:5–24.

Searles, H. (1963), Transference psychosis in the psychotherapy of chronic schizophrenia. In: *Collected Papers on Schizophrenia and Related Subjects*, 1965, pp. 654–716.

_____ (1973), Concerning therapeutic symbiosis. *Ann. Psychoanal.*, 1:247–262.

_____ (1975), The patient as therapist to his analyst. In: *Tactics and Techniques in Psychoanalytic Therapy, Vol. II*, ed. P. Giovacchini. Northvale, NJ: Aronson, pp. 95–151.

_____ (1978–1979), Concerning transference and countertransference. *Internat. J. Psychoanal. Psychother.*, 7:165–188.

_____ (1979), *Countertransference and Related Subjects*. New York: International Universities Press.

Shapiro, L. (1996), The embodied analyst in the Victorian consulting room. *Gender & Psychoanal.*, 1:297–322.

Shapiro, T. & Emde, R., ed. (1991), Affect: Psychoanalytic perspectives. *J. Amer. Psychoanal. Assn.*, 39(Sup.).

Simmel, G. (1984), *George Simmel: On Women, Sexuality and Love*, ed. & trans. with introduction by G. Oakes. New Haven, CT: Yale University Press.

Spezzano, C. (1993), *Affect in Psychoanalysis*. Hillsdale, NJ: The Analytic Press.

Stern, D. (1983), Implications of infancy research for psychoanalytic theory and practice. *Psychiat. Update*, 2:7–21.

_____ (1985), *The Interpersonal World of the Infant*. New York: Basic Books.

_____ (1992), Commentary on constructivism in clinical psychoanalysis. *Psychoanal. Dial.*, 2:331–363.

Stewart, H. (1989), Technique at the basic fault/regression. *Internat. J. Psycho-Anal.*, 70:221–230.

Stolorow, R. & Atwood, G. (1992), *Contexts of Being: The Intersubjective Foundations of Psychological Life*. Hillsdale, NJ: The Analytic Press.

_____ Brandchaft, B. & Atwood, G. (1987), *Psychoanalytic Treatment: An Intersubjective Approach*. Hillsdale, NJ: The Analytic Press.

Stone, L. (1961), *The Psychoanalytic Situation*. New York: Oxford University Press.

Strachey, J. (1934), The therapeutic action of psychoanalysis. *Internat. J. Psycho-Anal.*, 15:127–159.

Szasz, T. (1963), The concept of transference. *Internat. J. Psycho-Anal.*, 44:432–443.

Tansey, M. & Burke, W. (1989), *Understanding Countertransference: From Projective Identification to Empathy.* Hillsdale, NJ: The Analytic Press.

Tauber, E. (1954), Exploring the therapeutic use of countertransference data. *Psychiatry,* 17:331–336.

Thompson, C. (1964), Ferenczi's relaxation method. In: *Interpersonal Psychoanalysis: Papers of Clara M. Thompson,* ed. M. R. Green. New York: Basic Books, pp. 67–82.

Thompson, R. (1990), Emotion and self-regulation. In: *Nebraska Symposium on Motivation.* Lincoln: University of Nebraska Press, pp. 367–467.

Tomkins, S. (1962), *Affect, Imagery Consciousness.* New York: Springer.

Tower, L. (1956), Countertransference. *J. Amer. Psychoanal. Assn.,* 4:224–255.

Wallerstein, R., ed. (1992), *The Common Ground of Psychoanalysis.* Northvale, NJ: Aronson.

Whipple, D. (1986), Discussion of "The merits and problems with the concept of projective identification" by Janet Finell. *Psychoanal. Rev.,* 73:121–128.

Winnicott, D. (1960), Ego distortions in terms of true and false self. In: *The Maturational Process and the Facilitating Environment.* New York: International Universities Press, 1965, pp. 140–152.

_____ (1969), The mother–infant experience of mutuality. In: *D. W. Winnicott: Psychoanalytic Explorations,* ed. C. Winnicott, R. Shepherd & M. David. Cambridge, MA: Harvard University Press, 1989, pp. 251–260.

Index